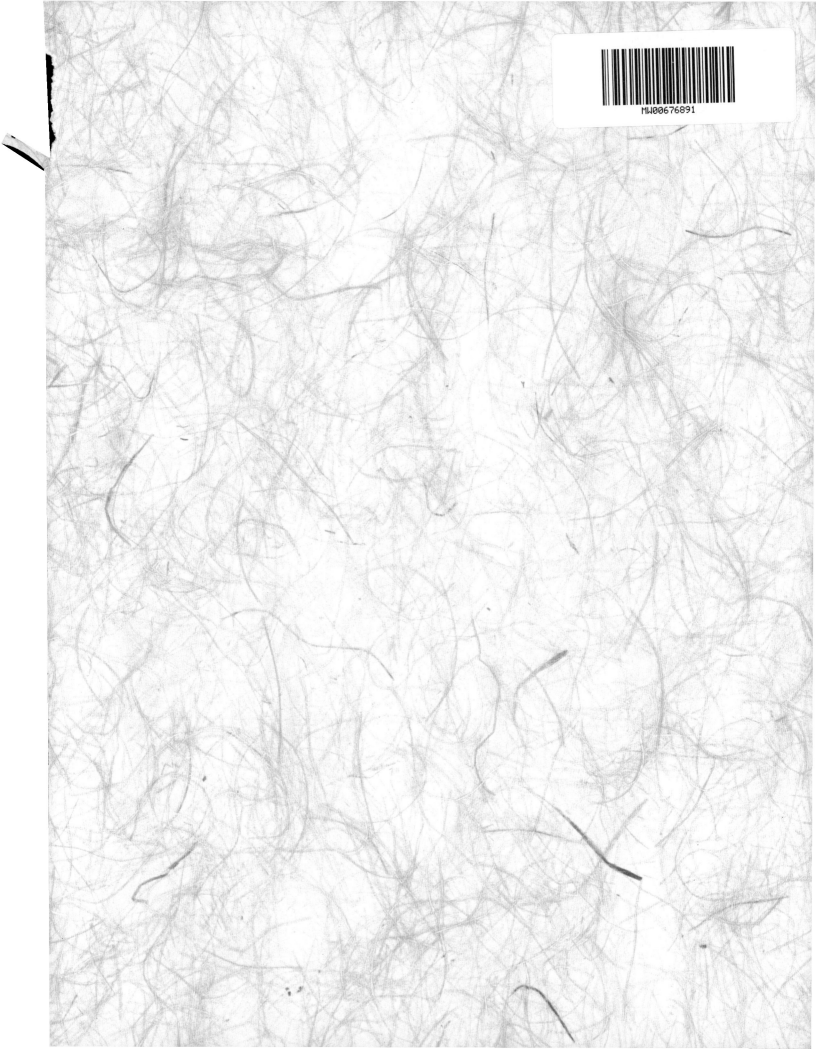

MW00676891

200 Years of Playtime Pottery and Porcelain

Lorraine Punchard

4880 Lower Valley Road, Atglen, PA 19310 USA

Dedication

This book is dedicated to the private collectors who were so gracious to welcome me into their homes to photograph and write about their collections. A special thank you, Paula Gerdes who lives in the Netherlands and has shared enormous amounts of information. My appreciation also goes out to Dorothy Amburst, Sara Austin, Nancy Callis, Judy Conn, Kay Curtis, Barbara Holzhauer, Ann Landgrebe, Pat Medlin, Joe & Margaret Randel, Patricia L. Smith, Marjorie Taylor, Sue Wagner, Joan Winn, Mary Ann Wise, and Marie & Cal Wylie.

Copyright © 2003 by Lorraine Purchard
Library of Congress Control Number: 2003100474

Designed by Joseph M. Riggio Jr.
Type set in Korinna BT / Aldine721 LtBT

ISBN: 0-7643-1814-4
Printed in China
1234

Published by Schiffer Publishing Ltd.
4880 Lower Valley Road
Atglen, PA 19310
Phone: (610) 593-1777; Fax: (610) 593-2002
E-mail: Info@schifferbooks.com
Please visit our web site catalog at **www.schifferbooks.com**
We are always looking for people to write books on new and related subjects. If you have an idea for a book, please contact us at the above address.

This book may be purchased from the publisher.
Include $3.95 for shipping.
Please try your bookstore first.
You may write for a free catalog.

In Europe, Schiffer books are distributed by
Bushwood Books
6 Marksbury Avenue
Kew Gardens
Surrey TW9 4JF England
Phone: 44 (0) 20 8392 8585
Fax: 44 (0) 20 8392 9876
E-mail: Bushwd@aol.com
Free postage in the UK. Europe: air mail at cost.

Contents

Introduction

Welcome to the world of children's play dishes. There are endless play dishes that have not been recorded. Many fine sets are in the hands of private collectors who have graciously consented to have them published in this book.

Sets of children's play dishes were intended for a specific purpose, such as a tea set or a dinner service set, just as dishes were designed for adults. Their size depended on the intended use. Larger sets were meant to be used by little girls for having parties for their friends and practicing the social graces of the times. Smaller sets were made for little girls to have parties with their dolls, or for their dolls to have parties among themselves. Therefore, the smaller sizes were often referred to as "doll dishes." However, there is still a smaller size, usually referred to as miniature or dollhouse size. One standard dollhouse size is one inch to the foot.

The search for the factories that made children's play dishes is never ending because other sets will always be surfacing. There is no way of knowing what companies made children's play dishes or how many, until sets are found and recorded.

My purpose is to determine the country of origin of a piece by the shape of the mold, decoration, and material used, such as porcelain or pottery. Pottery is earthenware that is fired and glazed. Other names used to describe pottery include semi-porcelain, soft-paste, opaque china, best body, new stone, and china stone. France uses the term half-porcelain. To determine porcelain, hold a piece to the light and you will see your fingers through its translucent body, whereas earthenwares are opaque.

It is important to learn to compare shapes, sizes, covers, finials, embossing, and base rims to help determine the manufacturer or country of origin and to date a set. One company could register a pattern and continue making it for many years, changing the decoration as often as they wished, which makes it hard to match dishes made over one hundred years ago. Some earlier sets were not marked but, as it became profitable, the same company added their name to their product. If the toy dishes were not intended for export they didn't have to be trademarked.

Early sets were often hand-painted, or transfers, or hand-painted over transfers. In later sets stenciling was applied through a cutout pattern, which was simple to do and could use unskilled labor. By the late 1800s most decorations were decals. A gold number on the base is the guilder.

According to the taste and means of a family, children's playtime dishes were a smaller scale of family china. Grading ranged from fair to exceptionally fine. In 1890 you could buy sets from five cents to five dollars. The number of pieces in a set varied as much as its price. Tea sets usually came packaged in two, four, or six place settings, with or without plates.

In 1891, Congress passed the McKinley Tariff Act. This required that goods imported to the United States be marked "Made In Country of Origin." Not every piece was marked and some used paper labels. To use the term "antique" an item should be at least one hundred years old, any less than that is considered a collectible.

Dates of wars play an important role in the manufactured goods of a country. The United States imported large quantities of children's dishes from Europe and England prior to World War I (1914-1918). Japan became the chief exporter of children's play dishes between the two World Wars until 1941, and again after World War II, which ended in 1945. Items marked Occupied Japan will date between 1945-1952.

United States pottery companies produced sets from the late 1800s to World War I, with very few sets produced after that. The Akro Agate and Depression Glass companies manufactured glass sets for children's dishes during the 1930s and 1940s. Tin dishes were popular from the 1920s to the 1980s. Plastic has been the material used most often since the 1950s.

Pricing sets of dishes is very difficult. Remember this is only a guide. Prices are determined by supply and demand and vary in different parts of the country. Another change that effects the prices is selling or buying at on-line auction sites where prices are inconsistently high or low. Prices should be lower for any missing pieces, chips, cracks, or repairs.

China salesman's samples are quite rare. Most small plates were made as toys. In England, John Mortlock, Callard & Callard and Thomas Gibson were known to make a china business card with their name on the front of the plate.

This little plate, 2 7/8 inches in diameter, has "RICHARD STANWAY / NEWCASTLE STAFFS" printed on the front of the plate. The reverse inscription:

CLOTHING
MANUFACTURER
CONTRACTOR & RETAILER
GENTLEMAN'S MERCER
HATTER &c
1879

This was most likely intended as an advertising give-away, or considered a trade card. With a hole in the top center, it was probably sewn to a garment.

Another style of a salesman's sample plate shows the different colors that were used to decorate china ware. The back is impressed "DRIE KLOKKEN" meaning "three bells" in Dutch. The little plate is 3 inches in diameter. Each number stands for a different color. 24035 is dark green, 20044 is yellow, 22018 is red, 20029 is orange, 24046 is light green, 24045 is medium green, 24042 is dark blue, 21049 is pink. It is interesting to see this type plate in miniature rather than adult size.

Austria

Pottery and porcelain toy dishes were produced in Austria in the nineteenth and twentieth century. Carlsbad was known as Karlsbad after World War I when that section of Austria became part of Czechoslovakia. This area was a center for porcelain factories.

"VICTORIA, CARLSBAD, AUSTRIA" is trademarked on these serving pieces. It is very nice porcelain decorated with little pink flowers and green leaves. The mold has designs in relief with fancy handles. It would date between 1880s and 1910. The shapes are unique, oval on one end and flat on the other. The cover is a half lid. $150-200. More information on Victoria, Karlsbad is in the Czechoslovakia section.

Teapot is 5" high,
Creamer and covered sugar bowl.

"VICTORIA, AUSTRIA, BLUE BIRD" is the information on the trademark. It would date about 1900. It is a lovely porcelain set decorated with blue birds and blue rims. $300-400.
    Teapot 3.62" high,
    Creamer and open sugar bowl,
    Four cups and saucers 3.25" diameter.

"Austria" is marked on this jardinière along with a printed mark. A jardinière is a large ornamental vessel to hold cut flowers or a potted plant. This one is nicely decorated with blue flowers and green leaves with little touches of gold. $75-125.
    Pedestal 3.5" high,
    Bowl 2" high,
    Both pieces are 5.5" high.

An impressed beehive mark is the trademark for Austria. A lazy susan is an interesting piece to add to a table setting. These four earthenware pieces fit on the metal holder. They are decorated with a floral design and raspberries. It is not a quality item. $35-50.
    Four dishes 3.12" at widest,
    Metal holder 3.37" high.

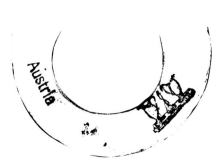

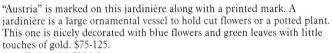

Belgium

"Fabrique Impériale et Royale de Nimy, Nimy, Belgium" is on the black trademark. This mark was used from 1921 to 1951. This set dates from about 1940. It is made of thick earthenware with hand-painted decoration. $200-300.

 Teapot 5.5" high,
 Creamer and open sugar bowl,
 Six cups and saucers 5" diameter.

Mouzin, Lecat & Cie. in Nimy, Belgium, is the maker of this junior size dinner set, made between 1898 and 1920. The trademark is in green and yellow. This set is made of earthenware, decorated with roses and leaves transfers. There is gold on the handles and rims. According to Belgium's custom it has only one covered vegetable dish. $700-900.

 Covered soup tureen with stand 5.87" high,
 Vegetable dish with cover,
 Salad bowl,
 Gravy boat with attached underplate,
 Two meat dishes in different sizes,
 Two pickle plates, diamond-shaped,
 Fruit dish on high stand,
 Six soup plates 5.5" diameter,
 Six dinner plates 5.5" diameter,
 Six dessert plates 4.75" diameter.

China

Chinese Export is a term used to describe the Chinese porcelain wares that came from China. These wares were made for export. The color of the porcelain has a gray tint with tiny pits in the surface. From 1784 to about 1835 the United States imported wares directly from China. There are no examples in this book. Please see *Playtime Pottery and Porcelain from Europe and Asia.*

There are new sets, made for export, being produced in China at this time.

This small oriental tea set on a tray is trademarked like some Chinese marks dating around the turn of the twentieth century. The set has a dark maroon background with an oriental scene. The decoration is an outline transfer then hand-painted in enamel colors. It is interesting to have a matching tea-caddy. $200-300.
 Tray 5.62" diameter,
 Teapot 2.62" high,
 Four handless tea bowls,
 Tea-caddy 2.62" high.

This oriental tea set is not trademarked. It could be from China, Japan, South Korea or Thailand. It is celadon, which is a sea-green stoneware. The teapot and tea bowls fit on the matching tray. The stoneware was made to have crazing and then was glazed. Tea bowls are handleless so that when the cup is too hot to hold the tea inside is also too hot to drink. $300-400.
 Tray 1.37" high by 7.75" diameter,
 Teapot 2.75" high,
 Tea bowls 1" high by 2.12" diameter.

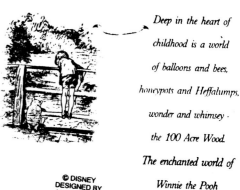

Deep in the heart of
childhood is a world
of balloons and bees,
honeypots and Heffalumps,
wonder and whimsey -
the 100 Acre Wood.
The enchanted world of
Winnie the Pooh
and his friends.

Winnie the Pooh is a favorite storybook character for children. This small sized set is trademarked "©Disney, Designed by Midwest of Cannon Falls." The warning on the box is "This is not a toy, not intended for use by children. Reproduced by Midwest of Cannon Falls, Made in China." It is based on the *Winnie the Pooh* works, Copyright A.A. Milne & E.H. Shephard. This is a new set from the 1990s. It is cream color pottery with soft pastel colors. The story is about boy named Christopher Robin and his toy animal friends, Winnie the Pooh, Tigger, Piglet, Rabbit and Eeyore in the Hundred Acre Wood. $25-50.

    Teapot 3.5" high,
    Creamer and sugar bowl,
    Two plates 2.75" diameter
    Two cups and saucers 2.25" diameter.

CLASSIC
POOH
© Disney

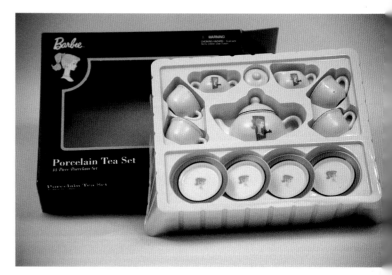

The Barbie ® doll was created by Mattel's company founders, Ruth and Elliott Handler in 1959. The Ken doll came out in 1960. Barbie was named after their daughter and Ken after their son. The information on the box reads "BARBIE, and associated trademarks are owned by and used under license from Mattel, Inc. ®2001 Mattel, Inc. All rights reserved." "More fun from Schylling, Made in China." The serving pieces and plates have a picture of Barbie's head with blond hair. Saucers were not included with this set. $13-15.

    Teapot 2.75" high,
    Creamer and covered sugar bowl,
    Four plates 2.5" diameter,
    Four cups.

"Made In China" is printed on the little tea set. It is a small size with a tray. There are hundreds of these small porcelain tea sets in many different molds from China, Taiwan and Thailand. They are sold in gift shops and catalogs around the country. They are nicely made and come in a variety of sizes. $20-50.

    Tray 6.25" diameter,
    Teapot 4.25" high,
    Creamer and sugar bowl,
    Two cups and saucers 2.25" diameter.

Czechoslovakia

For centuries Bohemia was a kingdom. Bohemia was a country of central Europe bounded on the south by Austria, the west by Bavaria, the north by Saxony and Lusatia, and east by Silesia and Moravia. In 1918, after the first World War, Bohemia, Slovakia, and Silesia formed an independent republic whose name is now Czechoslovakia. Therefore any pottery and porcelain marked Czechoslovakia would date after 1918. In 1918 Bohemia became the westernmost province of Czecho-slovakia. After the first world war Carlsbad, Austria, became part of Czechoslovakia. In 1930 more than thirty porcelain factories in the Carlsbad region formed the "Porcella." Before 1918, wares from the Victoria factory were marked, "Victoria, Austria." After that date, they were marked "Victoria, Czechoslovakia." Wares marked Bohemia would date before 1918.

The dishes range from finely crafted porcelain, to earthenwares, to a heavy, crude pottery.

This Circus set is trademarked "Victoria, Czechoslovakia" dating about 1930. There are interesting decals of circus scenes. This mold was manufactured with numerous different decorations. In the book *Playtime Pottery and Porcelain from the United Kingdom and the United States*, page 111 on the bottom is pictured an English royalty set using the same mold. It is unmarked and most likely was a special order from England to mark this event or this mold was bought by an English firm. See Austria for another Victoria set. $150-250.
   Teapot 4.75" high,
   Creamer and open sugar bowl,
   Two cups and saucers 3.25" diameter.

This set is marked "Victoria, Czechoslovakia." After the war, this Austrian factory became part of Czechoslovakia dating after 1918. The fine porcelain is iridescent, decorated with the flag from Hungary. $250-350.
   Teapot 6" high,
   Creamer 3.5" high,
   Open sugar bowl 2.12" high,
   Six cups and saucers 4.75" diameter.

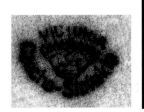

"MADE IN CZECHOSLOVAKIA" is printed on these pieces from about the 1920s to 1930s. It is made in fine porcelain. The decorations include a little girl with a Golliwog doll and a dog, a girl with a Golliwog and a doll, and a girl with an umbrella pulling a toy dog on wheels. $200-300.
　Teapot 4" high,
　Creamer 2.5" high,
　Open sugar bowl.

Bakers Chocolate began at the Walter Baker mills in Dorchester and Milton, Massachusetts. They have been making and selling chocolate and cocoa products since 1780. They also had a large assortment of bonus premiums that have been very collectable for many years. Advertising items included trays, cans, silver items, celluloid fans, linen tea cloths, glass ash trays, cookbooks, bookends, pencil sharpeners, paper items and some china. The familiar trademark is the chocolate girl. In 1872 the chocolate girl became the registered trademark. It was taken from a pastel drawing of Anna Baltauf (1740-1825) who was a waitress in a Vienna chocolate shop. Royal Doulton, Dresden and Meissen made lovely cocoa pots. Other cups and saucers were commissioned by well-known china makers. As far as the articles written, there were no give-away premiums designed specifically for children.

"Made in Czechoslovakia" is printed on the base of these pieces. Anything marked Czechoslovakia would date after 1918, and this set would date from about the 1930s. It is earthenware decorated with a heavy black band and lighter blue band. There is also blue on the handles and her dress. She has brown hair. The striking feature on this set is a version of the head of the chocolate girl. $450-550.
　Serving pot is 6.75" high,
　Creamer 3" high, plus head makes it 4" high,
　Covered sugar to top of finial is 3" high,
　Six cups 2" high, plus head 3" high,
　Six saucers 4.5" diameter.

This coffee set is trademarked "Victoria, Czechoslovakia." It has unusual decals of a yellow car with green fenders, and another scene includes a boy and girl on a motorcycle. It is decorated with caramel luster trim. This set would date from the 1920s. $350-450.
    Coffee pot 6.25" high,
    Creamer 4" high,
    Sugar 3.25" high,
    Six cups and six saucers 4.25" diameter.

"Victoria, Czechoslovakia" is on the printed trademark. This is a very nice porcelain service that could be used for either tea or coffee. It may be a demitasse set rather than made for children's play. The colors are orange and black. $300-400.
    Serving pot 6.5" high,
    Creamer and sugar bowl,
    Two cups and saucers 4" diameter.

"CZECHOSLOVAKIA" is impressed in this crude pottery tea set. The background is blue-gray with dark maroon rims. The center decoration is a little boy with a red shirt on a brown pony. This type of soft pottery chips easily. $100-125.
    Teapot 4.75" high,
    Creamer and sugar bowl,
    Four plates 5.5" high,
    Four cups and saucers 4" diameter.

"CZECHOSLOVAKIA" is impressed in the base. It is the country of origin for this crude pottery tea set. It is cream colored with a center hand-painted decoration of a rabbit. Green trim and birds complete the scene. This type of pottery would chip or break quite easily. It would date about the 1930s. $125-175.

    Teapot 5.25" high,
    Creamer and covered sugar bowl,
    Four cups and saucers 3.5" diameter.

This dinner set was made in Czechoslovakia by Wegea circa 1930. The quality of the porcelain on this dinner set is very good and it is pure white. The subject of the decals are children playing, and toys. It is finished with gold trim. This large dinner set is called junior size, so children could have really used it to eat their dinner. $400-500.

Covered soup tureen 5.87" high,
Vegetable dish with cover,
Meat platter,
Gravy boat with attached underplate,
Salad bowl,
Six soup plates 5.5" diameter,
Six dinner plates 5.5" diameter.

"CZECHOSLOVAKIA" is impressed in this soft pottery tea set. The swan and cattail decoration is all hand-painted in a heavy raised paint. Each swan is a little different. The teapot and sugar bowl each have a swan on both the front and back. It is glazed over the painting. The color is dark brown with dark green rims on the sugar bowl cover, plates and saucers. $150-200.

    Teapot 5" high,
    Creamer 3.75" high,
    Covered sugar bowl,
    Four plates 5" diameter,
    Four cups and saucers 3.5" diameter.

"Karlsbad" is written in gold letters on the face of each piece. The country of origin would be Czechoslovakia dating after 1918. The wide border is all gold with hand-painted enamel flowers in pink or blue with green leaves. It is a smaller sized but very attractive. $150-250.

Tureen 4.12" high,
Platter 4.25" long,
Four serving dishes,
Compote,
Five plates 3.25" diameter.

"CZECHOSLOVAKIA" is the marking on the candlestick. It is lovely porcelain decorated with holly and berries. Czechoslovakia factories produced some very fine porcelain and glass. $35-65.
Candlestick 3.75" high,
Base 2.25" diameter.

Czechoslovakia is the country of origin for this Blue Onion pattern dinner set. There is a "Certifikat" that came with the set. It is dated the 4th day of November 1994. It is well made in heavy porcelain. Included with the set are two place mats and two matching napkins. $200-300.

Tureen and lid 3.5" high,
Platter 4.5" long,
Two serving dishes,
Two plates 3.5" diameter,
Two plates 2.5" diameter,
Two soup plates 3.25" diameter.

Denmark

Denmark's industrialization escalated in the 1870s. One of Denmark's advantages was their trading seaport center, located between Scandinavia and Germany with shipping routes around the world. The two major porcelain factories are Royal Copenhagen and Bing & Grondahl.

Bing and Grondahl factory was established in Copenhagen, Denmark in 1853. Grondahl was the technical and artistic person while the Bing brothers supplied the money and developed a market for chinaware. Bing and Grondahl produced the first Christmas plate in 1895. The firing and glaze process used at Bing and Grondahl gives the porcelain a unique appearance. It has a very smooth feel with light shading in the glaze. These little plates are trademarked "B & G, Copenhagen Porcelain, Made In Denmark, Design Antoni – 4901-337," "4902-337," "4904-337," 4906-337." These four little plates are 3.5 inches in diameter. They have two little holes in the back for hanging. $50-75.

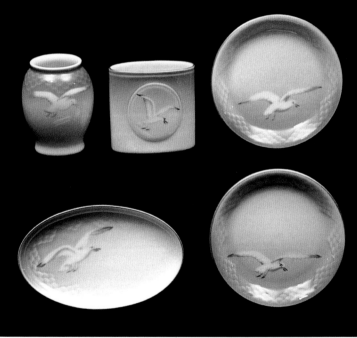

"B&G, Copenhagen Porcelain, Made in Denmark" is the information on the trademark of these fine porcelain pieces. There are two different marks, the three towers mark dates after 1962 and the circle mark dates after 1970. These pieces were not made as children's pieces but are the right size to be used as children's play dishes. This is the seagull pattern, which is all hand-painted. The pieces have a blue shaded background with gold rims and little touches of gold on the seagulls. Each piece $35-50.

Oval piece 2.5" high,
Vase 2.75" high,
Platter 2.75" by 4.5"
Two plates 3.75" diameter.

England

English play dishes are very interesting because potteries began making toys for the public around 1770 and English craftsmen used a better system for marking their wares than did potters of most other countries. This helps collectors of today determine the manufacturer and the issue date of a given set. Thanks to Geoffrey A. Godden for his book *Encyclopaedia of British Pottery and Porcelain Marks,* which identifies the maker, location, and date.

In 1910 the Staffordshire district, known as The Potteries, combined six towns to make one city called Stoke-On-Trent. These towns included Tunstall, Burslem, Hanley, Stoke-upon-Trent, Fenton, and Longton. Some of the well-known factories located in this area are Wedgwood, Spode, Minton, Coalport, Royal Doulton, and Mason's. Besides the well-known factories, there were hundreds of small factories. The local raw materials (clay and coal) and the canals to ship the goods played a major part in establishing the pottery industry here.

Children's Staffordshire sets were made for the export trade from the late 1700s to the present time. Early sets were decorated by hand painting or transfers. Transfer patterns were designed on a copper plate then copied on tissue paper and pressed on the pottery wares before firing. The monochrome colors were usually blue, red, green, and brown. The trademark was printed with the transfer so it is the same color as the decoration. Sometimes hand-painting was applied over the glaze to enhance the set. Luster, an iridescent glaze in different colors, decorates some sets. In the late 1800s decals became an easy and colorful way to decorate the china.

When one manufacturer produced dishes that were popular to the public, other pottery firms copied either the molds or the decorations. Other factors that help determine the set's origin and date are the shape of the pieces, particularly serving pieces, base rims, handle, cups, and saucers. Most dish sets from the Staffordshire district are earthenware, which is pottery with a glaze. They often develop crazing, the small cracks on the surface glaze. Unlike porcelain, earthenware sets are opaque. Porcelain is fired at a high temperature to become glass-like and bone china is porcelain that has added animal bone in the clay to produce a very white base.

In England, play dishes were produced in sets intended for a specific purpose. A majority of the dishes found are tea sets. The sets should include a waste bowl.

In England this was referred to as a "slop basin," and was used as a receptacle for cold tea, or the dregs of tea before refilling a cup with fresh tea. There is no one rule that holds consistently true pertaining to children's wares. An early tea set that includes four or six cups and saucers often has only one or two serving plates and a waste bowl. English tea sets seem to have an unlimited number of shapes and styles. A nicely matched set includes cups and waste bowl with the same basic shape in different sizes. Another good point to remember in sizing features is that the height of the teapot is close to the diameter of the plates or saucers.

The next most popular sets are the dinner services. These do not include cups or saucers as water or milk was the most likely drink to be served with a meal for children. Some manufacturers also produced some very special sets such as dessert services and fish sets, but they are extremely hard to find.

Generally, "England" alone was used in the marks from 1870 to 1891. From that year on, stipulations of the McKinley Tariff Act required that goods imported into the United States from England bear the words "Made In England." Articles so marked can be dated as originating from 1891 on but there are exceptions. For example, a big importer ordering large quantities directly from England may have received unmarked pieces mixed in an order. Goods not intended for export but bought by tourists or immigrants may not be marked at all. Also, goods shipped today from England to Canada are only marked "England."

Here are some tips for dating pieces. From 1780-1810, teapot and sugar bowl lids fit over the top, not recessed. Teapot drum or bulbous shapes with high necks are common. The handles and finials are quite plain. Teapot spouts are straight or have a slight curve. The cream pitchers have a pointed or very wide lip. The base rims are thin. They often have a pearlware glaze.

Between 1815-1835, London shape (rectangle) is common. See examples in the pages that follow. Hand-painted decorations or Adam Buck transfers are often used. Adam Buck refers to an artist (1775-1833) known for his drawings of ladies and children dressed in the Empire fashion. His prints were used for transfers on dishes.

Between 1820-1840, bulbous and oval shapes are common. Recessed covers are used. Some handles and finials are more decorative. The sugar bowls are almost the same size as the teapot. Sets have large waste bowls and a wide lip on the creamer. Mostly transfers are used.

Between 1840-1860, almost all the Flow Blue sets are produced. A lot of individual styles are used with fancy handles and finials. Waste bowls are still large.

Between 1850-1880 taller teapots are popular. Many factories are beginning to scale down the intricate work. Waste bowls are getting smaller.

Between 1880-1900 Charles Allerton produces large amounts of dishes. The earthenware is heavier with flatter bases. Manufacturers decorated with transfers and started using decals.

From 1900 on, sets are decorated mostly with decals. There are still a lot of individual styles. Cups are quite plain. Some nice bone china sets were made.

Josiah Wedgwood opened a pottery factory in Burslem, England in 1759. Local reddish-brown clay burned black in firing, a term we now call black basalt. Wedgwood's black stoneware was introduced in 1768. This set is marked "WEDGWOOD" dating the set 1770s to 1780s. Please take note of the unique shapes on all the pieces. The early sets had one set of saucers to be used for either tea bowls or coffee cups. It is remarkable that this set survived with so many pieces and in excellent condition. $7500-8500.
Tea stand 2.5" high, by 3.25" top diameter,
Teapot 2.5" high, glazed on the inside,
Creamer glazed on the inside,
Covered sugar bowl,
Tea caddy with original cover,
Large waste bowl,
Three cups with handles,
Five tea bowls,
Three saucers 3.25" diameter.

"Wedgwood" is impressed on the base of this set, made about 1820. "Black basalt" is the name given by Josiah Wedgwood to describe his black stoneware. He named it after the hard black rock that was much sculpted by the Egyptians. This set is decorated with engine-turned patterns. These were incised when the piece was "leather-hard" (partially dry) with engine-turning lathes. This way you can get a repetitive pattern, cut with the aid of a guide tool. The extra pieces are called a tea and coffee infuser. It was the forerunner of the filter method coffeepot, invented in 1803. It could be used for either coffee or tea. $1200-1400.
Teapot 2.75" high,
Creamer and sugar bowl (missing cover),
Waste bowl,
Filter 2.12" high by 2.5" diameter,
Strainer 1.87" diameter,
Pounder 1" high by 1.5" diameter.

"Wedgwood" is impressed on these cane basketweave serving pieces dating about 1830. The teapot is 2.5 inches high and is glazed on the inside. The creamer is glazed on the inside. The sugar bowl has no glaze. Glaze was needed if liquids were used to prevent soaking into the pottery. $300-400.

"Wedgwood" is the impressed trademark on this tea set, dating it between 1860 and 1891. The set is made of a high-fired, dense, stoneware body tinted by a yellow-buff color and decorated with bas-relief work in green that was applied by hand. The outside is not glazed, but the inside is glazed to hold the liquid. "Jasperware" is the name given by Josiah Wedgwood in 1777, to describe his invention. Jasperware comes in a lot of colors but the blue and white are the most popular. In the center of the finial on the lids is a little hole because the lids were made on an engine turned lathe. The hole in the teapot's lid doubles as a steam hole. $300-400.
   Teapot and cover 2.5" high,
   Creamer and covered sugar bowl.

"Wedgwood" is impressed on this serving pot. In the Netherlands this is known as a chocolate kettle. The hot chocolate, made of cocoa, hot milk, and sugar, was prepared in the kitchen, poured in the kettle and then served. The handle of this kettle is made of wicker with a black band woven through it. The earthenware kettle has a recessed cover with a steam hole in the center of the finial. $300-400.
   Chocolate kettle and cover 3.25" high.

This Yorkshire Prattware tea set would date about 1790. The set is in excellent condition. It is decorated with hand-painted baskets and flowers. In England the names of the pieces are a teapot, covered sugar bowl, milk jug, slop basin and tea bowls. The saucers are deep-dish style with handless cups called tea bowls. $4000-5000.
   Teapot 4.37" high,
   Creamer and covered sugar bowl,
   Waste bowl 2.25" high by 4.25" diameter,
   Six cups and saucers 4" diameter.

This canary yellow glazed earthenware teapot, cup and saucer would date about 1800 to 1820. It has a recessed cover and a straight teapot spout. The pattern is "single rose." At some time in the past the handle had been broken and someone added a tin handle. It adds character to the set. $700-900.

Teapot 3.12" high,
Cup and saucer 4.25" diameter.

England produced some of the earliest tea sets that we find today. This set is decorated with dark blue transfers in an oriental design. The bases of the pieces have deep narrow rims. The saucers have the deep bowl style. It includes a large waste bowl. All the features would date early 1800s. $1200-1400.

Teapot 3.25" high,
Creamer and covered sugar bowl,
Large waste bowl,
Six cups and saucers 3.75" diameter.

Tea sets from 1790 to 1810 are scarce and difficult to find. Some of the nice features of this era include a cover fitting over the top of the teapot, a tall neck, one deep dish saucer with handless cup, and of course all hand-painted. These are the only pieces in this set, but it is a very nice example of the early wares. $350-400.

Teapot 4" high,
Cup and saucer 4" diameter.

"HACKWOOD" is impressed on the base of the teapot and sugar bowl. There were four Hackwood manufacturing combinations located in Hanley between the years 1827 and 1843. The color is sky blue. It has interesting mold shapes and has been engine turned for decoration. $250-350.

Teapot 2.5" high,
Covered sugar bowl.

This porcelain tea set is decorated with background transfers of a tree and ground cover with birds. There are hand-painted details in silver luster over the birds and on the edge trim. Silver was used to make luster trim that comes out as a straw color after firing. With the type of porcelain, the double twisted handles, the bud finials and a serpent head on the teapot spout, it would probable date about 1830 to 1840. It is a quality set in excellent condition. $1000-1400.

    Teapot 5.25" high,
    Creamer and covered sugar bowl,
    Waste bowl, 2.75" high by 3.9" top diameter,
    Two serving plates 6" diameter,
    Five cups and saucers 4.25" diameter.

Some English Staffordshire tea sets are still found in a complete service. This is a London shape tea set with no trademark, dating about the 1830s. It is decorated with a green sheet pattern transfer. It has a similar mold to other sets in this time frame. The sugar bowl is still large compared to the creamer, because the sugar was more coarse than it is now. $800-1200.

    Teapot, 4" high,
    Creamer and covered sugar bowl
    Waste bowl 2.5" high, by 4.25" top diameter,
    Two serving plates 4.37" diameter,
    Six cups and saucers 5.6" diameter.

This English London shape tea set would date about 1820s to 1835. It is buff color decorated with Adam Buck prints in rust color. The green trim is hand-painted on the rims and finials. $700-900.

    Teapot 3.5" high,
    Sugar bowl,
    Large waste bowl 2.62" high by 4.5" diameter,
    One cup with ornate handle.

Dishes in the London shape date around 1835. This bone china set is decorated with a variant of the tea leaf design. It is larger than some of the play dishes. Look at the unusual shape of the waste bowl. $600-800.

    Teapot 3.5" high,
    Creamer 2.75" high,
    Sugar bowl 3.5" high,
    Large waste bowl,
    Four cups and saucers 4.5" diameter.

This mold has been used with a number of different transfers. The pieces are not trademarked. They are possibly John Ridgway 1830-1855. This set has a wide stylized border with checks and a floral drape. The light blue center transfer pictures a large pagoda-type building, with a tree and two people in the foreground. $700-800.

Teapot 4" high,
Covered sugar bowl,
Four handleless cups,
Three saucers 4.25" diameter.

"SCOTT" is impressed on each saucer. Southwick Pottery, Sunderland, Durham, used the "SCOTT" mark form 1838 to 1883. The style of the pieces should date the set about the 1840s. It is interesting to have a matching coffee pot and a tea pot in the same set. It is hand-painted with red and green designs. Early features on this set are the wide lip on the creamer, and the deep-dish saucers. $700-900.

Coffee pot 6.25" high,
Tea pot 3.75" high,
Creamer and covered sugar bowl,
Three cups and saucers 4.25" diameter.

This set uses the same mold featured in the previous set and is in a pattern called "Napier." In the *Dictionary of Blue and White Printed Pottery 1780-1880* by Coysh & Henrywood, they credit the pieces to John Ridgway 1830-1855. This child's set is unmarked but would date about 1840. It is decorated in an oriental pattern with a wide border, oriental buildings and floral design. In the center picture are two people in a boat. It was popular in English ceramics to use oriental designs. This is a partial set but a full set would average about $700-800.

Teapot 4" high,
Two handleless cups and saucers.

Luster is made by adding gold compound to the white body. Many different companies produced luster but Sunderland was noted for this type of decoration. The luster could range from pink to purple. This set is not trademarked but would date about 1835. This is a well-matched set with a band of pink luster and a deep purple luster design. The teapot and sugar bowl are both the same size in bulbous shape. The waste bowl has a nice rounded shape and the cups have straighter sides. This is a case where the waste bowl and cups are not matched shapes. $400-500.

Teapot 4.5" high,
Covered sugar bowl,
Waste bowl 2.5" high by 4" top diameter,
Six plates 5.12" diameter,
Six cups and saucers 4.87" diameter.

This tea set is unmarked. It has a unique handle on the teapot. It is Flow Blue with polychrome hand-painted over the blue. It has lovely shapes dating 1840s. The cups are handleless, the sugar bowl is almost as large as the teapot, and the creamer has a wide lip. It has two serving plates, which is a feature of early sets. $2500-3200.
    Teapot with cover 4" high,
    Creamer and covered sugar bowl,
    Five handleless cups,
    Five saucers 4.5" diameter,
    Two serving plates 4.75" diameter.

The English Registration mark dates this set Oct. 17, 1844. It is decorated in a light blue transfer. The wide border is stylized with a decoration on each side. The center is an abbey on the left with ruins on the right. There is a gondola in the foreground with five people. Some trees and foliage complete the setting. $500-600.
    Teapot 3.5" high,
    Sugar bowl,
    Waste bowl 2.5" high by 4" top diameter,
    Five cups and saucers 4.5" diameter.

This English tea set is unmarked but has the shapes of Spode wares dating about 1820s-1830s. It is decorated with dark blue transfers of two women in the center with a wide floral border. $700-900.
    Teapot 3" high,
    Creamer and sugar bowl,
    Two cups and saucers 4" diameter.

This English set would date about 1840. The green transfers include two swans in an outdoor setting with a wide floral border trim. $700-900.
    Teapot 4" high,
    Creamer and sugar bowl,
    Waste bowl, 2.5" high by 4.75" diameter,
    Two serving plates 4.87" diameter,
    Six cups and saucers 4.25" diameter.

This English Staffordshire set would date about the 1860s. It has black transfer scenes of children in military dress. The sugar bowl is large and the waste bowl is small. $700-900.

    Teapot 4.25" high,
    Creamer and sugar bowl,
    Waste bowl,
    Four plates 4.62" diameter,
    Four cups and saucers 4.5" diameter.

Pictured here are two more lovely sets in the same Minton mold as previously shown. The light blue set is decorated with a transfer in a stylized design. This set includes individual serving plates 4.25 inches in diameter.
The polychrome set has a transfer background in dark blue with flowers and leaves in reds, orange, blue, and green painted over. The only marking on the set is the decorators number 6771. The cups have different shape than the other two sets. All three Minton sets would be in the same price range.

Minton used this mold on children's play dishes about 1840's. They were decorated with transfers or transfers embellished with hand painting. This is a lovely set with birds and floral designs as the main theme. $500-700.

    Teapot 4.5" high,
    Creamer and covered sugar bowl,
    Two serving plates 5.5" diameter,
    Four cups and saucers 4.5" diameter.

This set is unmarked but believed to be from the Minton factory. It is bone china decorated with hand-painted enamel flowers and blue line trim. The aqua bands make the set stand out. The handles are double twisted. It would date around the middle of the 1800s. $700-900.

    Teapot 4.75" high,
    Creamer and covered sugar bowl,
    Waste bowl,
    Two serving plates 7.25" diameter,
    Four cups and saucers 4.35" diameter.

Minton is the maker of this fine bone china tea set dating around 1850. It is beautifully decorated in bright colors with the decorator's number 4804 on all the pieces. It has double twist handles and a lovely shaped serving plate. $700-900.
Teapot 3.75" high,
Creamer,
Waste bowl 2" high by 3.25" diameter,
Serving plate 5.37" diameter with handles,
Four cups and saucers 4.75" diameter.

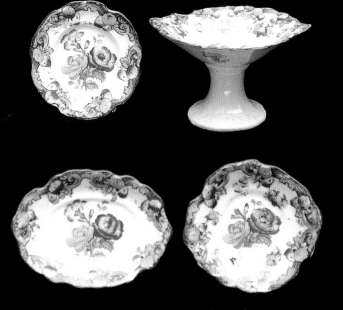

Francis Morley & Co. was located on Broad St., Shelton, Hanly from 1845 to 1858. Some of these pieces are impressed "F.M." The decorator's number, 4938, is on all the pieces of the tea, dinner, and dessert sets. It is very unusual to find three sets together intact and all by the same decorator. The black outline is hand-painted in greens, reds, and yellow. Three matching sets $3500-5000.
Teapot 4.5" high,
Creamer 2.5" high,
Sugar 3.5" high,
Waste bowl 4.5" top diameter,
Two plates 4.25" diameter,
Two cups and saucers 4.5" diameter.

Large tureen, cover, underplate 5" high,
Two smaller tureens, covers, ladles, underplates 3.75" high,
Covered vegetable dish 3" high,
Salad bowl 2" high,
Pie dish 2.25" by 3",
Butter boat with underplate 2" high,
Tree and well meat dish 3.75" by 5",
Four meat dishes 2.25" by 3" to 4.24" by 5.75",
Ten dinner plates 4.25" diameter,
Five soup plates 4.25" diameter,
Eleven pastry plates 3.25" diameter,
Eleven cheese plates 2.75" diameter.

Compote 3.25" high by 5.25" top diameter with handles,
Two round serving dishes 4.5" diameter,
Two oblong serving dishes 3.5" by 5",
Four plates 4" diameter.

Samuel Alcock was the maker of this fine porcelain tea set circa 1845. In Mr. Goddens book, *Encyclopaedia of British Porcelain*, this mold is pictured in an adult set with just the pattern number printed on each piece. This child's set has the same mold with the pattern number 1520 printed on each piece. This is an exceptionally beautiful porcelain tea set with exquisite hand painting in blue and pink, light green border trim, and gold accents. $1400-1800.

    Teapot 4.75" high,
    Covered sugar bowl,
    Waste bowl 2.5" high by 4.87" top diameter,
    Two serving plates 6" square,
    Six cups and saucers 4.75" diameter.

"ALCOCK" is the impressed name on this set but there is not enough information to identify the exact maker. The style of the pieces would date the set about 1840s-1850s. Some of the nice features include ornate handles, wide lip on the creamer, extra large waste bowl, in this nicely matched set. It is decorated with a light blue transfer. $700-900.

    Teapot 3.62" high,
    Creamer and sugar bowl,
    Waste bowl 2.37" high by 4.75" diameter,
    Two serving plates 5" diameter,
    Six cups and saucers 4.5" diameter.

Mellor, Venables & Co, Hole House Pottery was located in Burslem. They were in business from 1834 to 1851 and were probably the makers of this set. The set is marked "Ironstone" and is decorated with a marble pattern in mulberry color. It has vertical panels in a Gothic shape. Interesting features include handless cups, tall covers, squared handles, and a large waste bowl. $1800-2200.

    Teapot 6.5" high,
    Creamer,
    Sugar bowl 5" high,
    Waste bowl 3.25" high 5" top diameter,
    Four cups and saucers 4.25" diameter.

Samuel Alcock was the maker of this tea set dating circa 1845. It has the same mold as the previous set but has entirely different decorations. The background is medium blue, hand-painted in enamel colors using orange and green leaves. There is gold trim on the teapot spout, finials, handles, bases, rims and on the blue field. It is an exceptional set. $1400-1800.

    Teapot 5" high,
    Creamer 4" high,
    Sugar bowl 4.5" high,
    Two plates 4" diameter,
    Two cups and saucers 4.75" diameter,
    Cake plate 6.25" by 7".

Spongeware decorated sets are very desirable. This set is not trademarked, which is typical of these types of sets. It would date about 1840 to 1850. The serving pieces have octagonal shapes, recessed covers and a bud-type finial. The handless cups add character to the set. The spongeware is well applied in a blue color. Some other decorations may include an all over spongeware design. $1200-$1400.

Teapot 5.75" high,
Creamer and covered sugar bowl,
Two cups and saucers 4.24" diameter.

This early English Mulberry tea set came with handleless cups. It has a floral pattern. The set would date about 1840-1845. The serving pieces are octagonal, the cups have twelve panels and the saucers have sixteen panels. It is a lovely well-matched set. $1500-1700.

Teapot 4" high,
Creamer and covered sugar bowl,
Three cups and saucers 4.25" diameter.

"Ironstone, CORINTH, G. Phillips, Longport" is the information given on the trademark with a registration mark dating this set January 11, 1845. George Phillips was a Staffordshire pottery located in Longport from 1834 to 1848. The transfer decoration is blue. It depicts an outdoor setting with ancient buildings, and a waterway with a boat in the center. The border is a wide stylized design. The serving pieces are quite large with small handleless cups. $900-1200.

Teapot 5.25" high,
Creamer 3.5" high,
Sugar bowl 4.75" high,
Large waste bowl 4.75" diameter,
Four cups and saucers 4.36" diameter.

"ENGLAND" is the only marking on this tea set. It is a brown sheet pattern of flowers and stems. The sugar bowl is large compared to the rest of the set and is a lighter color so it may not have come with the set. The style is a good match. The set looks as if it would date about the 1880s. $600-800.

Teapot 4.12" high,
Creamer and covered sugar bowl,
Six plates 4.75" diameter,
Six cups and saucers 4.5" diameter.

The "E & F" trademark on this set stands for Elsmore & Forster, Tunstall of Clayhills Pottery. They were in business from 1853 to 1871. It is an ironstone set decorated with copper tea leaf design, copper bands and trim. It is a rare set to find. $1500-2000.

   Teapot with cover 5" high,
   Creamer 3.25" high,
   Covered sugar bowl 4.25" high,
   Waste bowl 2.25" high by 3.25" top diameter,
   Six cups and saucers 4.25" diameter.

Thomas Dimmock & Company used this impressed mark. The company was in business from 1828 to 1859. The decoration is a green sheet pattern with a border. There is a matching dinner service. $600-900.

   Teapot with cover 4" high,
   Creamer and covered sugar bowl,
   Four plates 5" diameter,
   Four cups and saucers 4.5" diameter.

"LADIES ALL, I PRAY MAKE FREE AND TELL ME HOW YOU LIKE YOUR TEA" is the caption on the front of the teapot. The center transfer on this teapot pictures three ladies having tea. This is an earlier mold from around the 1850s. $100-150.
   Teapot 3.75" high.

Thomas Dimmock, a Staffordshire pottery, was the maker of this tea set. It is impressed "Pearl Wear" and has a monogram mark which dates the set between 1828 and 1859. It is a striking set decorated with a stylized blue design and blue rims. It was typical to have two serving plates with four cups and saucers in this time period. $600-900.

   Teapot 4" high,
   Creamer and sugar bowl,
   Two plates 6" diameter,
   Four cups and saucers 4.5" diameter.

Bone china was used on very nice sets of dishes for children. This set should date after 1850, looking at the shapes and the quality. If a set is marked bone china it would date from the twentieth century. It has unusual tall finials, which are easy to hold. The set is decorated with hand-painted birds, green leaves and red berries. Gold trim and rims complete the decoration. $500-600.

    Teapot 5" high,
    Creamer 3" high,
    Sugar 4" high,
    Waste bowl 4.25" top diameter,
    Two serving plates 5.5" diameter to edge of handles,
    Four cups and saucers 4.25" diameter.

This blue and white earthenware set was registered August 23, 1848, but does not give the factory. The transfer design features two people in an outdoor setting with water, trees, buildings and mountains in the background. In the foreground, next to the people, stands a large urn. The border is wide with pictures of a castle. The handleless cups add character to this set. $400-500.

    Teapot 4.25" high,
    Creamer and covered sugar bowl,
    Six plates 4.25" diameter,
    Six cups and saucers 4.6" diameter.

"MOSS ROSE, B.H. & Co." is the information on the trademark. B.H. & Co. stand for Beech, Hancock & Co, Swan Bank Pottery in Burslem dating 1851 to 1855. It is English Staffordshire decorated with blue transfers of the Moss Rose pattern. It has a stylized border with large roses. Each serving piece has three feet. Included is the nice large waste bowl. $700-900.

    Teapot 4.5" high,
    Creamer and covered sugar bowl,
    Large waste bowl,
    Six cups and saucers 4.6" diameter.

This set is unmarked but believed to be an English mold from F. & R. Pratt & Co., High Street, Fenton, dating after 1850. The set has ornate molding and is nicely decorated. The scene shows two children riding in a goat cart with an attendant. It is said to represent royal children at Windsor Castle. $1000-1500.

    Teapot 4.75" high,
    Creamer 3.5" high,
    Sugar bowl 4.5" high,
    Waste bowl 4.5" top diameter,
    Six plates 4.75" diameter,
    Six cups and saucers 4.5" diameter.

Similar footed shapes were produced by John & Robert Godwin 1834-1866, Turner & Tomkinson 1860-1872 and Ralph Hammersley & Son 1860-1905. This Staffordshire set is unmarked, but is closest in shapes to Ralph Hammersley, dating around the early 1860s. It is white earthenware decorated with red bands and red accents on the handles. $400-500.
 Teapot 4" high,
 Creamer and covered sugar bowl,
 Waste bowl,
 Two plates 4.75" diameter,
 Four cups and saucers 4.35" diameter.

Copeland, Spode Works, Stoke, was a Staffordshire pottery using this mold with different decorations. The impressed Copeland mark with a crown was used from 1847. It is an elegant set decorated with brown transfers in a stylized pattern. The body is cream colored. It has an exceptional waste bowl. The creamer has a pointed lip. $400-600.
 Teapot 3.87" high,
 Creamer and covered sugar bowl,
 Large waste bowl,
 Two serving plates 5" by 5.5",
 Two cups and saucers 4.5" diameter.

This marble Flow Blue set is unmarked but has the shapes of Thomas Dimmock & Company, dating 1828 to 1859. It has a large waste bowl and ornate handles. $1800-2500.
 Teapot 3.87" high,
 Creamer and sugar bowl,
 Waste bowl 2.87" high by 4.5" diameter,
 Six cups and saucers 4.5" diameter.

The back stamp gives the pattern name "PANAMA" on this set made by T & S. Impressed in very small letters is "Opaque China, Barker & Till" This is a Stafford-shire pottery from Sytch Pottery in Burslem, dating 1846-1850. It is earthenware decorated in a green sheet pattern. The shapes are unique. The teapot and sugar bowl have eight sides with recessed covers and lovely finials. $300-$500.
 Teapot 5.25" high,
 Covered sugar bowl,
 Two serving plates 4.75" diameter,
 Five cups and saucers 4.5" diameter.

This bone china tea set is decorated in an oriental theme. There is a transfer that has additional hand-painted details in touches of blue, green, and red. This set is dated around 1880s with the smaller waste bowl. Oriental wares were popular and the English imitated their work. $600-800.

  Teapot 4.12" diameter,
  Creamer and sugar bowl,
  Waste bowl 2.25" high by 3.5" diameter,
  Two serving plates 6.75" diameter with handles,
  Six plates 5.62" diameter,
  Six cups and saucers 4.37" diameter.

Sponged ware is Staffordshire pottery made for the cheapest market. Another term used is spatterware. This three-piece set is decorated with blue spongeware. A red flower and green leaves complete the center decoration. This type of set would date around the 1850s. $300-400.

  Teapot 4.75" high,
  Covered sugar bowl,
  One saucer 4.25" diameter.

A green seaweed transfer design decorates this tea set. It has a wide border with a center design, dating it about 1850. The set includes a large waste bowl, and a wide lip on the creamer. $700-900.

  Teapot 3.5" high,
  Creamer and covered sugar bowl,
  Waste bowl,
  Two serving plates 5" diameter,
  Four cups and saucers 4.5" diameter.

"Scotts Bar" is the name of this Flow Blue pattern circa 1850. It is quite a simple pattern but interesting when seeing the set together. It has nice finials and a small waste bowl. $1000-1500.

  Teapot 3.5" high,
  Covered sugar bowl,
  Waste bowl,
  Serving plate 5.12" diameter,
  One cup and saucer 4.5" diameter.

This Flow Blue set is decorated with a dahlia flower design. Gold is hand-painted over the blue. The mold shapes are the same as Allerton wares. Charles Allerton & Sons, Park Works, Longton began this Staffordshire Pottery in 1859 and this company was in business until 1942. This set should date about the late 1870s to early 1880s. The later wares that were trademarked "Allerton" usually date from the later 1880s. $1200-1500.

    Teapot 4.25" high,
    Creamer and sugar bowl,
    Four plates 5.5" diameter,
    Four cups and saucers 4.5" diameter.

This attractive English tea set would date about 1850-1860. It is decorated with dark cobalt blue transfers in a sheet pattern. It has a large sugar bowl and waste bowl. $500-700.

    Teapot 3.75" high,
    Creamer and sugar bowl,
    Waste 2.5" high by 4.25" diameter,
    Two serving plates 6.5" diameter,
    Four cups and saucers 4.25" diameter.

Another English set with no marking, other than the decorator's number, is in bone china. It is decorated with little hand-painted pink flowers, green leaves, and green accent trim. The taller pear-shape teapot and smaller waste bowl would date this set about 1860s. This is a partial set. $150-250.

    Teapot 5.25" high,
    Creamer,
    Waste bowl 2.5" high by 3.75" top diameter,
    Two serving plates 6" diameter.

The impressed mark is a square with "Best, L.P. & Co." for Livesley Powell and Co. Hanley, England. This mark would date the set between 1851 and 1866. This is a pear-shaped teapot and sugar bowl in a blue transfer using a "Hopberry" pattern. $200-250.

    Teapot 5.25" high,
    Sugar bowl,
    Waste bowl, 2.5" high by 3.75" top diameter,
    Two cups,
    One plate 4.87" diameter.

BEST
L. P. &
Co.

English Staffordshire companies produced large amounts of children's play dishes that do not have trademarks. This set has a red sheet pattern dating it about 1860. It has well matched shapes with a bud finial. Red wares are scarcer than blue, green, or brown. $400-500.

Teapot 5.5" tall,
Creamer and sugar bowl,
Waste bowl top diameter 4.5",
Six plates 5.25" diameter,
Six cups and saucers 5" diameter.

Staffordshire dishes came in many qualities. This set is a softer paste and would have been fired at a lower temperature than better quality sets. After all, this was a mass-produced toy. It is decorated in a brown stick pattern. It also came in red, green and blue. The date would be about the 1880s to 1890s. It is interesting to see the sugar bowl almost as large as the teapot, but the waste bowl is smaller than in earlier sets. $250-350.

Teapot 5.6" high,
Creamer and covered sugar bowl,
Waste bowl 2.25" high by 4.25" top diameter,
Four plates 4.25" diameter,
Four cups and saucers 4.5" diameter.

The potteries in the Staffordshire district produced numerous play dishes in the late 1800s. This set is typical of that time period. The tall teapot and large sugar bowl are almost the same size. The smaller creamer matches the shapes. It is decorated with red transfers. $300.400.

Teapot 5" high,
Creamer and covered sugar bowl,
Five plates 5.25" diameter,
Two cups and saucers 4.25" diameter.

"Bisto, England" is the trademark for Bishop & Stonier, Hanley. This Staffordshire pottery used this mark under this name from 1891 to 1939. The decals are all wooden Dutch dolls known as Peg Woodens or Penny Woodens . $400-500.

Teapot 3.5" high,
Creamer and open sugar bowl,
Two large plates 4.25" diameter,
Four plates 3.25" diameter,
Four cups and saucers 3" diameter.

This English bone china tea set came in the original box marked "Toy Tea Set." It has pretty decals with "Dollys Doctor" or "Dollys School" on each piece. It would date early 1900s. $300-500.
   Teapot 3.5" high,
   Creamer and open sugar bowl,
   Four plates 3.5" diameter,
   Four cups and saucers 3.5" diameter.

"H. S. & H." Stands for Holmes, Stonier, & Hollinshead, located in Hanley, Staffordshire. This partnership was in business between 1875 and 1882. This set has a nice registration mark dating it January 15, 1881 with the pattern name "AVONA." This set is decorated with brown transfers. The center scene is a windmill. The lid of the teapot has a deep inset. The teapot spout and handles have a bamboo style. $400-500.
   Teapot 4.75" high,
   Creamer and covered sugar bowl,
   Waste bowl,
   Six plates 5.12" diameter,
   Six cups and saucers 5" diameter.

"ALLERTONS, WILLOW, MADE IN ENGLAND" is the information given on the trademark. This mark was used between 1929 and 1942. Red Willow is more unique than blue or any other color. $300-500.
   Teapot 4.5" high,
   Creamer 2.75" high,
   Open sugar 1.6" high,
   Four plates 6.75" diameter,
   Four cups and saucers 4.5" diameter.

"COPELAND, SPODES ITALIAN, ENGLAND" is the printed trademark. This type of mark would date after 1891. Around the top rim of the teapot is the saying "We'll tak' a cup O' kindness yet for Days O' Auld Lang Syne." The blue transfers include scenes with castles and foliage, a shepherd man with a dog and sheep. The finial is a lion lying down. The shapes are unique. $500-700.
   Teapot 3.5" high,
   Creamer 3" high,
   Open sugar bowl,
   Waste bowl 3.75" top diameter,
   Two plates 4.5" diameter,
   Two cups and saucers 4.5" diameter.

"CAULDON, ENGLAND" is on the trademark. Cauldon Ltd, was located in Shelton, Hanley, from 1905 to 1920. It was a Staffordshire pottery. This set features shapes of much earlier wares. It is nicely decorated with blue transfers of a man standing in a Roman chariot pulled by a white horse, with foliage in the background. $400-600.

Teapot 3.75" high,
Creamer and open sugar bowl,
Four cups and saucers 3.75" diameter.

"Ridgways, Stoke-on-Trent, England" is the information given on this tea set. It is a blue sheet pattern. Ridgways produced a great number of sets in this mold with different decorations. They date in the late 1800s. $300-500.

Teapot 3.5" high,
Creamer and sugar bowl,
Six plates 4.5" diameter,
Six cups and saucers 3.5" diameter.

An impressed circle in a triangle is the only mark on this tea set. It is in a similar pattern as a known Powell and Bishop dinner set, dating this set between 1876 and 1878. The teapot has a replaced lid. It is decorated with transfers in light brown with hand painting over the transfers on all the pieces. $350-450.

Teapot 3.75" high,
Covered sugar bowl,
Two serving plates 5.18" diameter,
Six cups and saucers 4.5" diameter.

"England" is the only marking on this set. It is a mold that was used by Ridgways, dating it around the 1880s. The colors are bold reds and blues. $300-500.

Teapot 3.5" high,
Creamer and open sugar bowl,
Four plates 4.5" diameter,
Four cups and saucers 3.5" diameter.

ENGLAND

These five teapots are from the Ridgway Factory, Stoke-On-Trent. They would date from the 1880s. They are shown together to highlight the different decorations on the same mold as the previous tea sets.

The teapot with a basket of fruit is only marked "ENGLAND." It could be from another factory as it is a little larger.

The green and blue teapots on the top row are "Maiden Hair Fern" pattern, registered in 1881. The tip of the spout on the green teapot had been damaged and someone added a metal tip.

The floral teapot has soft colors. The name of the pattern is "HAMP-TON." The mark is from 1905.

The brown teapot is "Chintz," registered in 1882. The Chintz also came in blue, red, green and sepia.

The price range for each complete set would be $300-500.

Salt glaze is stoneware that was glazed by throwing salt into the kiln. They usually date around the 1880s. Salt glaze teapots with pewter tops were produced using different molds. Sometimes colors were added, such as blue or brown. This teapot is 4.75 inches tall in an off-white color. $100-150.

This set is similar in style to wares by Royal Doulton, Lambeth, England, but the potting is not as fine and the pieces are heavier. It is stoneware in a gray color, decorated with a blue band and black floral transfers. It has a row of beading on both sides of the blue band. Just above the spout is written "HILDA." The neck on the creamer and teapot are tall, the cover fitting over the top rather than recessed is an early 1800s style. $150-200.

Teapot 4.25" high,
Creamer,
Open sugar bowl.

The Charles Allerton Co. produced tons of play dishes that were exported to the American market. This is a standard shape used by this company. There are four other known shapes. The decoration is an oriental scene in red transfers. $300-500.

Teapot 5.25" high,
Creamer and sugar bowl,
Six plates 5.62" diameter,
Six cups and saucers 4.5" diameter.

This three-piece salt glaze set is buff color pottery dating around 1830s. It has deep embossing on all the pieces. It features ornate handles and nice finials. $200-300.

    Teapot 3.5" high,
    Creamer & sugar bowl.

Torquay Motto Wares were established during the years 1870 to 1900 and continue to the present time. This tea set would date early twentieth century. This tea set is not trademarked. It is decorated in the "Scandy" pattern. The back of the teapot reads "Have another cup full." The open sugar says "Take a little sugar." The cream pitcher has been added and is a little darker than the other pieces. On its back is "Demsher Craim, Jak an try et." The back of the cup says "Its very refreshing." $300-500.

    Teapot 3" high,
    Creamer and open sugar bowl,
    One cup and saucer 3.75" diameter.

"WATCOMBE, TORQUAY ENGLAND" is printed on the back of this set's pieces and one piece has "WATCOMBE, DEVON MOTTO WARE, REG NO, ENGLAND." Torquay is from South Devon, England. These wares were made from the red terra cotta clay found north of Torquay. The Watcombe Pottery was producing pottery from about 1901 to1962. The style of the thatched cottage between trees was called "Devon Motto Ware" or "Cottage Ware." "On the front of each piece is the cottage and on the back is a saying. Each piece is hand-painted and they all vary in the decoration. The sayings include "It's very refreshing" on the teapot and two cups. The back of the sugar bowl says "Take a little sugar," and the creamer says "Straight from the cow. The other two cups have "Take a cup of tea." The four plates each have a saying: "Actions speak louder than words," "Little boy blue come blow your horn," "Old Mother Hubbard went to the cupboard," "Jack and Jill went up the hill." $600-800.

    Teapot 3.25" high,
    Creamer and open sugar bowl,
    Four plates 4.5" diameter,
    Four cups and saucers 4" diameter.

Torquay Motto Wares came in a variety of patterns and colors. This set is decorated with a kingfisher under the glaze. It is blue with brown handles, rims, teapot spout and lid. The back of the teapot says "Have Some More Tea." The plates say "Help Yourself." $300-500.

    Teapot 3.75" high,
    Four plates 4.25" diameter,
    Four cups and saucers 4" diameter.

Other pieces in Torquay include a Crown Dorset Cottage miniature stein. This is an extremely rare piece. The saying on the back is "Come an zee us in th' zummer." It is 3.75 inches high. $400-500.

    The wild rose miniature plate is 4.5 inches in diameter. The back information is "Made In England." The background is deep purple with a rose flower and green leaves. $100-200.

These are small samples of Torquay pottery. They may have been children's pieces or just small pieces. They were made in England and Scotland. Torquay potters were Aller Vale 1891-1924, Hart & Moist Exeter about 1900 and on, Royal Torquay Pottery 1905-1940, Longpark Pottery 1903-1957, Watcombe Pottery 1901-1962, Devon Tors, Bovey Tracey 1920-1939, Babbacombe Pottery about 1952, St. Marychurch Pottery 1964-1968, and Dartmouth Pottery 1948. The most common patterns were "Scandy," "Cockerel," "Ship," and "Cottage."
Each piece $50-150.

    The Cockerel cup has three handles and is 2 inches high. The saying is "Better do one thing, than dream all things."
    The Cockerel creamer is 2.75 inches high, "Be aisy with the cream."
    The Ship jug is 3.25 inches high, "Drink like a fish, water only."
    The bowl is 3.25 inches diameter, "Niver zay die, up man an try."
    The Scandy bowl is 2.5 inches in diameter.
    The "PIN TRAY" is 2 by 4 inches.

Mason's began business in the early 1800s. Charles James Mason patented "Patent Ironstone China" in 1813. The Mason Company is famous for their ironstone. Mason's oriental patterns have been popular for over two hundred years. "England" added to the mark dates the pieces after 1891.

These three pieces have the Mason's mark with "England" so they were made after 1891 but they are in the old style. This was sold as a children's set but it is probably from a breakfast set. The sugar bowl is large for a child's set, but smaller than an adult sugar bowl. It is decorated in the old style with black castle transfer scenes and orange transfer trim. $200-250.

    Water pot 5.5" high,
    Sugar bowl 4.25" high,
    Creamer 3" high.

Here are more Mason's Ironstone pieces. The top three pieces and the bottom left have the earlier mark dating after 1820, probably 1845 to 1854. They are all decorated with oriental designs. The first pitcher and bowl have dark green trim with a red trademark. The second pitcher has a black transfer with hand-painted colors over the transfer, and a black trademark. The pitcher on the bottom left has a cobalt blue design with orange flowers hand-painted over the transfer, and a blue trademark. These three pitchers are about 3 inches tall. The old pitchers are about $100-150 each. The bottom center pitcher has a dark green main color with yellow leaves and gold trim. It has a green trademark and is 3.5 inches high. The bottom right pitcher is rust color with gold trim and has the same color rust trademark. It is 2 inches high. The last two pitchers were purchased in the 1990's. $50-75.

"Wedgwood, Eturia, England" is the trademark on this item. The plate is out of a tea set dating after 1891. There is no name for this pattern but it looks like a tall chimney for a pottery and people working around the area. This mold was also used on a Willow tea service. Tea set $300-500.
Plate 4.25" diameter.

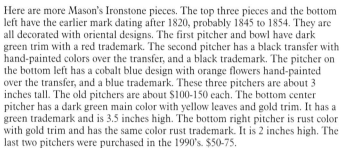

The information given on this small doll-sized tea set is "MASONS" with a crown, "Made In England" and "Mandalay" is the pattern name. The colors are attractive with dark blue and polychrome. They were produced in the 1990s. $100-150.
Teapot 3.12" high,
Two plates 3" diameter,
One cup and saucer 2.5" diameter.

"ATLAS CHINA, STOKE-ON-TRENT, ENGLAND" is the printed trademark used by Atlas China Co., Ltd. Atlas Works, Wolfe Street, Stoke. This trademark was used from 1906 to 1910. It is a well-crafted bone china tea set. The figures are Kate Greenaway designs of children. Kate Greenaway was a famous illustrator (1846 to 1901). She created designs of quaint, graceful, fascinating children. She had a feeling for original designs, color, and landscape. Her unique style of drawings brought about change in children's fashions. The craze was to copy slim Empire gowns, sashes, puffed sleeves with lace or ruffles and sunbonnets of the Kate Greenaway girls. Her drawings were used on china from England, the United States, and Germany, as well as other countries. This mold also has many different decals that would be valued at a little less than Kate Greenaway. $500-700.
Teapot 4.25" high,
Creamer and open sugar bowl,
Six cups and saucers 4" diameter.

Felix the Cat is the theme of this character set. "Shell, Made In England" is the trademark, dating this set about the 1920s. Felix the Cat was created by Pat Sullivan in 1917. It was featured in animated cartoons, sound cartoons, comic strips, and comic books. Some of the sayings on this set include "Now Felix Keep On Walking," "Felix Takes A Walk," "Will You Walk With Felix?" $400-500.

    Teapot 3.75" high,
Creamer and sugar bowl,
Four plates 4.25" diameter,
Four cups and saucers 3.75" diameter.

In 1893 the English lady Beatrix Potter wrote an illustrated letter to a child, Noel Moore, which told the adventures of a naughty little rabbit called Peter. Several years later she used the story for her first book, *The Tale of Peter Rabbit*. This book, and the twenty-two books that followed, became one of the most popular children's series in the world.

This set shows Peter Rabbit in seven different scenes of that story. The blue trademark gives the maker as Grimwades, Upper Hanley, England. It is from the 1920s in excellent quality porcelain. The decals are magnificent with gold trim finishing the decorations. $300-400.

    Teapot 3.75" high,
Creamer and open sugar bowl,
Two serving plates 6.25" diameter,
Four plates 4.12" diameter,
Four cups and saucers 4.5" diameter.

"Wedgwood" is impressed on this set and "Wedgwood, Eturia, England" is printed on the base. It is decorated with a blue transfer then hand-painted with green grass, caramel luster castles, and a man dressed in red who is fishing. Red rims complete the decoration. $300-400.

    Teapot 4.25" high,
Creamer and open sugar bowl,
Four cups and saucers 4.5" diameter.

"WEDGWOOD® of Etruria & Barlaston, Made In England, Copyright Frederick Warne & Co., PETER RABBIT" is the information on the trademark. This set is from the 1980s. The sayings on the face of the pieces include: "Now run along, and don't get into mischief," "I am going out," "Once upon a time there were four little Rabbits," "He jumped up and ran after Peter," "Peter sat down to rest; he was very damp with sitting in that can," "Peter never stopped running or looked behind him til he got home to the big fir-tree." $100-200.

    Teapot 4.25" high,
Creamer and open sugar bowl,
Two plates 4.25" diameter,
Two cups and saucers 3.25" diameter.

"PETER RABBIT, ©Frederick Warne & Co. 2001, WEDGWOOD, MADE IN ENGLAND" is the information on the trademark. It is a quality set made by the Wedgwood Company. The sayings are on the pieces. The front of the teapot has "Peter was a very naughty rabbit." The back of the teapot reads "He ran straight away to Mr. McGregor's garden." The creamer pitcher says "Where's Peter Rabbit?" The open sugar bowl says "Peter Rabbit hid in a watering can." The cups say "Peter Rabbit." The saucers read "Peter ran straight away to Mr. McGregor's garden, first he ate some lettuce, and then some radishes." The plates say "First he ate some lettuces, and some French beans; and then he ate some radishes." $100-125.

    Teapot 4" high,
    Creamer and open sugar bowl,
    Two plates 4.25" diameter,
    Two cups and saucers 3.25" diameter.

These pieces are Crown Staffordshire in the same pattern and with the same registered number 724202 as a play tea set. These pieces date 1928, but this is child's size, which could be part of a breakfast set. In any case it is beautifully made and decorated with hand-painted hollyhocks, leaves, and butterflies in enamel colors over a cream body. $100-175.

    Teapot 5.5" high,
    Plate 6" diameter.

These five spoon rests are trademarked "The World of Peter Rabbit © F.W." It features Peter Rabbit crawling under Mr. McGregor's garden gate and other scenes from the story of Peter Rabbit. $75-125.
    Spoon rests 3.75" by 1.62" diameter.

"CROWN DUCAL WARE, ENGLAND" is the trademark for the Company A.G. Richardson & Co., Ltd. located in Tunstall, dating this set between 1925 and 1930. The large flowers in the foreground are hollyhocks by a stairs and railing in an outdoor setting. It is nicely colored, with a blue sky shaded to green then brown at the bottom. Hollyhocks and other flowers are in the foreground with a country home in the background. This may have been a demitasse set or part of a breakfast set. It seems a little large for a child's set. $300-400.

    Coffee pot 6.75" high,
    Creamer 2.75" high,
    Open sugar bowl,
    Four cups and saucers.

"E.P.C., EMPIRE WORKS, STOKE-ON-TRENT" is the trademark. This is from the Empire Porcelain Co., a Staffordshire pottery using this mark from 1912 to 1928. The decals are sporting bears. They are playing golf, cricket, soccer, and roller-skating. $400-500.

    Teapot 3.75" high,
    Creamer and open sugar bowl,
    Two cups and saucers 4.25" diameter.

The Three Bears is the theme on this tea set. It is unmarked but the mold looks like it was made in England. The sayings on the pieces are: "The Three Bears," "Goldilocks Finds The Porridge," "Goldilocks Tries The Chairs," "Who's Been Sitting In My Chair," "Who's Been Sleeping In My Bed," "The Three Bears Say Good Night." $300-400.

    Teapot 3.75" high,
    Creamer and open sugar bowl,
    Four plates 5" diameter,
    Four cups and saucers 4" diameter.

This bear set is unmarked but is using the same mold as other English sets of the 1920s. The set is earthenware decorated with decals of bears. The serving plate is porcelain. The pattern could be called the sports bears because they are playing soccer, golf, and cricket. $400-500.

    Teapot 4" high,
    Creamer and open sugar bowl,
    Serving plate 6" diameter,
    Six cups and saucers 3.75" diameter.

This set is trademarked "SHELL WARE, ENGLAND, OLD ENGLISH." It is a simplified version of the Willow pattern. It has an unusual border and gold rims. $200-300.

    Teapot 4" high,
    Creamer and large open sugar bowl,
    Four plates 5.25" diameter,
    Four cups and saucers 4.25" diameter.

"Real Staffordshire, Willow, H A & Co." is given on the trademark. The company is H. Aynsley & Co., Longton. They used this printed mark from 1946 onward. Over fifty companies in England produced a version of the Willow pattern. This set is lightweight with very dark blue transfers. Since this is a later set, the sugar bowl is an open style used for sugar lumps. $250-350.

Teapot 4.75" high,
Creamer and open sugar bowl.

"Wadeheath, By Permission, Walt Disney, England" is the information on the trademark. Wadeheath Ware began using "By Permission Walt Disney" in 1936. It is from the story of Snow White and the Seven Dwarfs whose film came out in 1937. Snow White and Dopey are featured on the teapot. The other dwarfs are pictured on the other pieces: Sleepy, Doc, Bashful, Happy, Grumpy, and Sneezy. The creamer depicts Bambi and the sugar bowl pictures Thumper. The film Bambi came out in 1937. $250-300.

Teapot 3.25" high,
Creamer and open sugar bowl,
Four cups and saucers 4 " diameter.

WADEHEATH
BY PERMISSION
WALT DISNEY
ENGLAND

"MADE IN ENGLAND BY WADE, HEATH & CO. LTD., MICKEY MOUSE NURSERY WARE, Manufactured by exclusive arrangement with Walt Disney-Mickey Mouse Ltd." is the information on the box of this set. There is a wonderful figural teapot of Donald Duck. Other decals are Mickey Mouse, Donald Duck, and Baby Seal. $300-400.

Teapot 4" high,
Creamer 2" high,
Open sugar bowl 2.5" high,
Two cups and saucers 4" diameter.

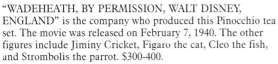

"WADEHEATH, BY PERMISSION, WALT DISNEY, ENGLAND" is the company who produced this Pinocchio tea set. The movie was released on February 7, 1940. The other figures include Jiminy Cricket, Figaro the cat, Cleo the fish, and Strombolis the parrot. $300-400.

Teapot 3" high,
Creamer and sugar bowl,
Two plates 4" diameter,
Two cups and saucers 3" diameter.

The shapes show that England produced this tea set about the 1930s. It is earthenware decorated with nursery rhyme decals and little sayings. $150-200.
"Mary Had A Little Lamb, Its Fleece As White As Snow"
"Little Jack Horner Sat In A Corner"
"Ride A Cock Horse To Banbury Cross"
"There Was An Old Woman Who Lived In A Shoe"
"Tom, Tom, The Pipers Son"
"Humpty Dumpty Had A Great Fall"

Teapot 3.75" high,
Creamer and open sugar bowl,
Four plates 4.5" diameter,
Four cups and saucers 4" diameter.

"Biltons, Made In England" is the printed trademark on this set. Biltons is a Staffordshire pottery located on London Road, Stoke. This mark was used after 1947. The color is pink with rings on the mold of the teapot, creamer and the outer rim of the plate. The wing-tip finial is typical of this time period. $200-300.
Teapot 3.5" high,
Creamer,
Four plates 4" diameter,
Four cups and saucers 3" diameter.

"NURSERY TEA WARE, MADE IN ENGLAND" is the information on the original box. There is no manufacturer's name on this set from about the 1930s. It is interesting that they would package a set for three. $125-200.
The names on the pieces include:
"The Queen of Hearts"
"Humpty Dumpty"
"Little Tommy Tucker Sings For His Supper"
"Ding, Dong Bell, Pussy's In The Well"
"Rock a Bye Baby In A Tree Top"
"Little Boy Blue Come Blow Your Horn."

Teapot 3.5" high,
Creamer and open sugar bowl,
Three cups and saucers 3" diameter.

"MADE IN ENGLAND" is the only marking on this tea set dating from the 1930s-1940s. It is nicely molded with decorations of a big red rose with green leaves. It has green border trim. The serving plate has little handles. $200-300.
Teapot 4.5" high,
Creamer and open sugar bowl,
Serving plate 5.5" diameter,
Four cups and saucers 4" diameter.

"OLD ENGLISH COTTAGE WARE" and "KEELE ST. POTTERY CO., LTD., MANUFACTURED IN STAFFORDSHIRE ENGLAND, HANDPAINTED" is the information given on the trademark. The company was located in Tunstall from 1913 to 1958. $150-250.
  Teapot 3.5" high,
  Creamer 2" high,
  Open sugar bowl 1.75" high.

Carlton wares in the colored floral and fruit embossed designs were popular in the 1920s and 1930s. The only marking is "1799" on the sugar bowl. The molds are nicely embossed, especially the saucers. The color is bright yellow with hand-painted orange flowers, green leaves and brown stem on the handles. $200-300.
  Teapot 3.25" high,
  Creamer and open sugar bowl,
  Two cups and saucers 4.12" diameter.

"Royal Winton, Made in England" is trademarked on this set. Also added in gold letters is "Gainsborough, CAN. RD. 1954." The company name is Grimwades LTD, Winton, Upper Hanley, and Elgin Potteries in Stoke. It is a Staffordshire pottery that began in 1900. Some earthenwares were marked Grimwades. This set is cream-colored earthenware with gold trim. It is decorated with decals depicting men and women in period costumes: a woman walking with a fruit basket; a woman spinning wool; a woman having her hair combed; a lady and a man walking; and a man sitting. The most interesting feature of this set is that it came with a toast rack. This may be part of a breakfast set rather than made as a child's set. $100-200.
  Teapot 4.25" high,
  Creamer and small open sugar,
  Toast rack 2.5" by 2.9".

George VI was the king of England from 1936 to 1952. This set was made to commemorate his coronation on May 12, 1937. The teapot, plates, cups and saucers picture George VI and Queen Elizabeth I. The creamer and sugar bowl feature the young Princess Elizabeth who would later become Queen Elizabeth II. This is a smaller sized set. $200-300.
  Teapot 3.25" high,
  Creamer and sugar bowl,
  Two plates 3.87" diameter,
  Two cups and saucers 3" diameter.

45

"Spode Copeland China, England" is printed on the trademark. This set was produced for the coronation of Queen Elizabeth on June 2nd, 1953. "ER" with a crown over the initials is featured on each piece. A floral border completes the decoration. It is a small doll-sized set in bone china. $200-300.

Teapot 2.25" high,
Creamer and sugar bowl,
Two plates 2.87" diameter,
Two cups and saucers 2.5" diameter.

"ALICE IN WONDERLAND" and "THE MAD HATTERS TEA PARTY" are printed on the face of this plate. It is from a set of children's play dishes whose cups are mug shape. It is twentieth century bone china with the following information on the back of the plate: "Manufactured for Harrods LTD, LONDON." Another manufacturer, Hammersly, also made a children's feeding bowl with "ALICE IN WONDERLAND" between the years 1912 and 1939. This plate is almost 6 inches in diameter. $20-30.

"COALPORT, Bone China, Made In England, Est. 1750, PAGEANT" is the information on this little miniature tea set. Coalport Porcelain Works have been located at Stoke-on-Trent since 1926. This mark was used after 1960. This set was packaged with the teapot, creamer, and sugar bowl in one box. A plate, cup, and saucer were packed in another box. $200-300.

Teapot 2.25" high,
Creamer and sugar bowl,
One plate 3" diameter,
One cup and saucer 2.5" diameter.

"WEDGWOOD" is impressed on these pieces. Jasper-ware is a dense white stoneware with metal oxides added for the color. This small set is blue jasper embellished with white cherub figures and swags. A cherub is without clothes as an innocent child, whereas an angel wears clothes. $100-200.

Tray 5" by 6.5",
Teapot 2" high,
Coffee pot 2.75" high,
Creamer and sugar,
Two plates 3" diameter,
Two cups and saucers 2" diameter.

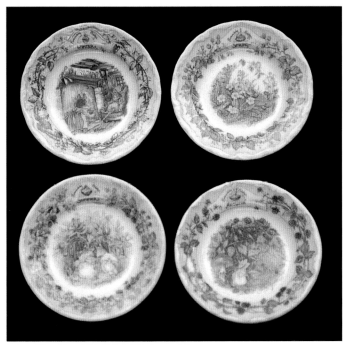

"DESIGNER, Hand Made, Staffordshire, Fine Bone China" is on the trademark. The tray says "Goosey Goosey Gander." There are titles of nursery rhymes on all the pieces. They include; "Jack Sprat Could Eat No Fat," "Little Miss Muffet," "Humpty Dumpty Sat On A Wall," "Old Mother Hubbard," "Baa Baa Blacksheep," "Doctor Foster Went To Gloucester," "Sing A Song Of Sixpence," and "Ride A Cock Horse To Banbury Cross." This is a new set from the 1990s. $75-125.

    Tray is 5 by 8.75",
    Teapot 3.25" high,
    Creamer and sugar bowl,
    Two cups and saucers.

"PORTMEIRION, BOTANIC GARDEN 25th Anniversary, 1972-1997." is the information given on this little commemorative tea set. Gray & Co. pottery was in business from 1912 to 1961 and then became Portmeirion in 1962. The Botanical series has been one of their best products and is very collectable. Also on the pieces is "Made in Britain, Designed by Susan Williams-Ellis." The botanical names of the flowers and their common names are on the pieces. $125-150.

    Narcissus Minimus – Small Narcissus
    Cyclamen Repandum – Ivy Leaved Cyclamen
    Lepidotum – Rhododendron
    Rosa Canina – Dogrose
    Viola Tricolor – Heartsease
    Bellis Prennis – Daisy
    Veronica Chamaedrys – Speed Well.
    Tray 7" round plus handles,
    Teapot 2.25" high,
    Two plates 2.12" diameter,
    Two cups and saucers 1.87" diameter.

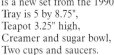

"BRAMBLY HEDGE" is the name on the front of this set's platter. The back trademark reads: "Royal Doulton, Tea Service, From the Brambly Hedge Gift Collection. They found Mr. Apple in the kitchen drinking mint tea with Mrs. Crustybread." "© Jill Barklem-1990." Each place setting stands for winter, spring, summer, and fall. The decals are little mice in different settings. The border is the brambly hedge. $75-125.

    Tray 6" by 10",
    Teapot 4" high,
    Creamer and open sugar bowl,
    Four plates 4" diameter,
    Four cups and saucers 3.5 " diameter.

Another set of Botanical designed flowers are on these pieces. They are from the 1990s. The teapot was sold separately and the six cups and saucers were sold in a box. These could be child's size or demitasse size. $150-200.

    Teapot 4" high,
    Six cups – all different flowers.
    Six saucers 4.62" diameter.

The Spode Company produced these 3.25 inch plates in the late 1990s from old patterns. The back of the plates includes the following information. Set $75-100.
    SPODE
    The Spode Blue Room Collection
    Georgian Series
    Reproduced from a hand engraved copper plate
    1. "Willow" – First introduced c.1790
    2. "Rome" – First introduced c.1811
    3. "Woodman" – First introduced c. 1816
    4. "Botanical" – First introduced c. 1820
    5. "Girl At Well" – First introduced c. 1822
    6. "Floral" – First introduced c. 1830

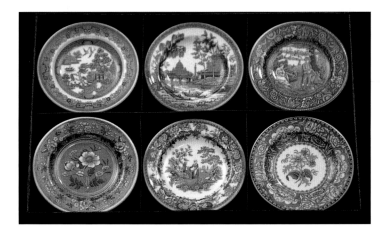

"Spode, Made In England, Christmas Tree" is the trademark on this set. The box has the following information: "Made in England, Imported by The Royal China & Porcelain Companies Inc., 1265 Glen Ave., Moorestown, New Jersey 08057." This is a new set from the 1990s. $100-200.

    Teapot 3.75" high,
    Creamer 2.5" high,
    Sugar 3" high,
    Two plates 4.5" diameter,
    Two cups and saucers 3.75" diameter.

Spode
Made in
ENGLAND
CHRISTMAS TREE
S3324-Z

16

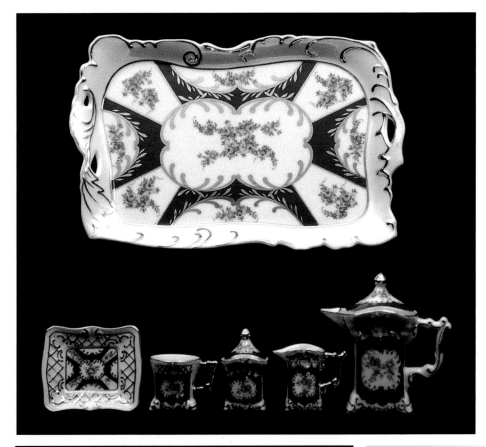

"Roselle, OCC & Co., STAFFORDSHIRE, ENGLAND" is the information given on the trademark. It is from the 1990s. The set is finely made in porcelain, and decorated with gold, royal blue and small floral designs. The embossing on the tray and saucers is hand-painted in gold. There are other sets from this company using different molds. $75-125
    Tray 7" by 11",
    Teapot 4.25" high,
    Creamer 2" high,
    Sugar 2.5" high,
    Two cups and saucers 2.5" by 3.2".

Another new Spode piece, made in England, is this platter in the Spode design "ITALIAN," which was first issued circa 1816. The size is 3.5 inches by 4.5 inches. $35-50.

Right and above right:
Lorna Bailey is an artist making new small tea and coffee services with a tray. They are trademarked "Old Ellgreave Pottery, Lorna Bailey Range, Hand Painted, Burslem, England." These sets are from the 1990s.
    The sets came with a tray 6" by 7.25", and each set has a name.
    The tea set name is "Pagoda Garden." The teapot is 2.25" high.
    The coffee set name is "House and Path." The coffeepot is 3" high.
    The saucers are 2.75" in diameter. $75-125 each set.

"WEDGWOOD" is impressed on each piece with the code letter "D" dating the set 1875. It is creamware, all hand-painted in enamel colors with green, blue, and red. Red borders complete the decoration. This set contains fifty-four pieces. $2200-2700.

> Tureen with cover 3.5" high,
> Two covered vegetable dishes 4.5" square,
> Seven meat dishes 3" by 4" to 4.5" by 5.75",
> Four pie dishes 2.5" by 3.25",
> Two open serving dishes 2" by 3",
> Oval serving dish 3.5" long,
> Small rectangle dish 2" by 3.25",
> Small ladle,
> Twelve dinner plates 4.25" diameter,
> Five soup plates 4.25" diameter,
> Fifteen smaller plates 3" diameter.

Wedgwood creamware came in a variety of sizes. This picture gives a better idea of sizes. The dinner plates are from four different sets. Their diameters are 3.25", 4.25", 6", and 7". The berry bowls vary in size and designs. The sauce pitchers or butter boats are from the same four sets. The two larger sets are the next two sets featured in this book.

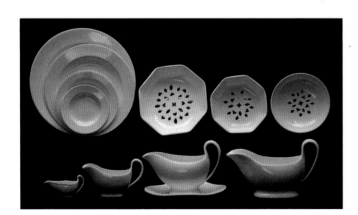

"WEDGWOOD" is impressed on all the pieces of this creamware set. There are code letters on the pieces dating from the late 1870s into the 1880s. This is a medium large set containing forty-two pieces, some of which are very unusual. Some of the mold shapes and finials were designed by Wedwood in 1817. $2200-2800.

> Large tureen, cover, stand 5.75" high,
> Covered vegetable dish 6" diameter, plus one vegetable base,
> Large dish with a drain lining 7" diameter,
> Fancy pedestal dish with embossing 4" by 6",
> Sauce pitcher with attached base 4" by 5.75",
> Square covered dish with underplate 4" by 6",
> Smaller covered dish with underplate 3.5" by 4.5",
> Two diamond shaped dishes 4" by 5",
> Round covered dish 2.75" diameter,
> Small salt dish 1.5" high by 2.25" long,
> Ten dinner plates 6" diameter,
> Six soup plates 6" diameter,
> Five smaller plates 5.25" diameter.

"WEDGWOOD" is impressed on each piece of this creamware dinner set. It is a large size intended for children to really eat their meals. It may be considered a junior set. The pieces have very nice flower finials. Three of the vegetable dishes have a steam hole in the center of the finial. The pedestal dishes have flower and leaves embossing by the open handles. Some pieces have the code "A" dating them in 1872. Other pieces have code letters from a few years later. The set contains 59 pieces. $2500-3000.

Large tureen, cover, stand, ladle 5" high by 7.5" wide,
Smaller tureen, cover and stand 4.5" high by 6.5" wide,
Sauce pitcher or butter boat 6" long,
Four covered vegetable dishes 6" diameter,
Two pedestal dishes 4.75" by 7",
Square covered serving dish 4.5",
Two small serving dishes with ruffled edges 3.75" by 5",
Two diamond-shaped dishes 5.5" by 6.5",
Two rectangle serving dishes 4.5" by 6",
Octagon serving dish 5.5" diameter,
Berry bowl with three feet 4.5" diameter,
Two large meat dishes 7" by 9.5",
Eleven dinner plates 7" diameter,
Twelve soup plates 7" diameter,
Six smaller plates 5.12" diameter.

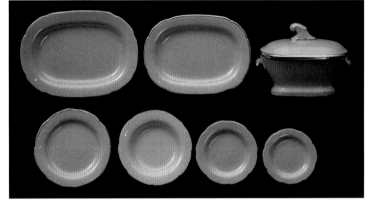

The beige color of this set is referred to as drab ware. It is non-porous stoneware that is sometimes glazed, such as these pieces. These pieces came from two partial sets and date around 1820. Some have a gold rim and others are plain. Each piece $25-75.

Covered tureen 3.5" high,
Two meat dishes 5" and 5.5" long.
Three plates 3.5" diameter,
Three plates 2.75" diameter,
Two soup plates 3.4" diameter,
One plate 2.35" diameter.

This small dinner service dates about the 1830s. It has the same shapes as the Kite Flyers, Monopteris, or Institution sets. It could have been made by Hackwood between 1827 and 1843. This is a partial set decorated in a blue sheet pattern. $700-900.

Large tureen cover 2" by 3.75",
Sauce tureen 2.5" high,
Covered vegetable dish,
Four meat dishes 2.5" by 3.25" to 3.75" by 5",
Pie dish 2.5" by 3.25",
Dinner plate 3" diameter,
Three soup plates 3" diameter,
Six pastry plates 2.75" diameter,
Two cheese plates 2.5" diameter.

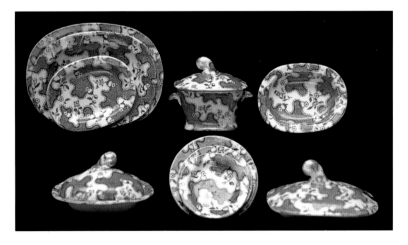

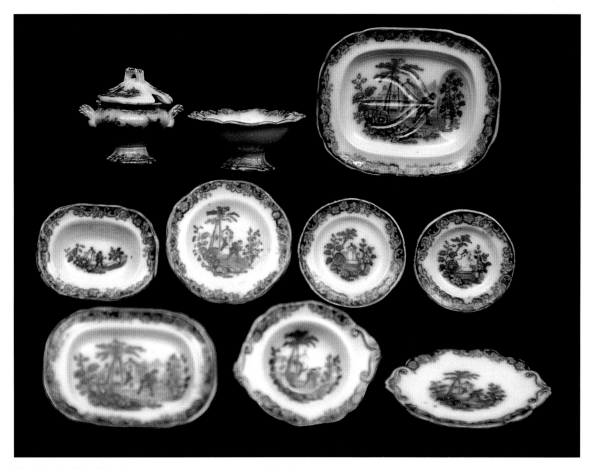

This English Flow Blue dinner set is unmarked but would date between 1840 and 1860. The Flow Blue is painted with polychrome. It depicts a man with a watering can watering flowers. The background includes foliage and a building. It has a floral border with hand-painted flowers. This set also came in plain Flow Blue. $3500-4000.

    Underplate for the large tureen 4.5" diameter,
Small tureen 3" high,
Salad bowl 1.75" high,
Two bases for vegetables 3.75" diameter plus one cover,
Two pie dishes 3" by 3.75",
Tree and well meat dish 4.5" by 5.75" diameter,
Three large meat dishes 4.25" by 5.5",
Three smaller meat dishes 4" by 5",
Six soup plates 3.5" diameter,
Twelve dinner plates 4" diameter,
Twelve pastry plates 3.25" diameter,
Twelve cheese plates 3" diameter.

This English Flow Blue dinner set is the same mold as sets from 1839. The Flow Blue transfer pattern is cut from a large sheet and fit onto the children's pieces. There is no border print. The whole set consists of fifty-two pieces. $3500-4500.

    Soup tureen and lid 3.75" high,
Underplate 5.12" long,
Two sauce tureens 2.75" high,
One underplate 3.75" long,
Covered vegetable,
Open serving dish, butter boat,
Salad bowl, pie dish,
Two pickle dishes,
Six meat dishes 4.4" to 6.9" long,
Six soup plates 4" diameter,
Twelve plates 4" diameter,
Six plates 3.25" diameter,
Six plates 2.75" diameter.

This dinner set is unmarked but has the shapes of Francis Morley, dating between 1845 and 1858. It is decorated with a blue stylized transfer border. The set was purchased from Australia with the following information:

"Original owner George Oliver Greathead. Apprenticed at a Staffordshire pottery in the 1840s. When his apprenticeship was complete he became a minor partner and as part of his duties traveled promoting wares from the pottery. Came to NZ (CHCH) in the mid 1850s. Wares from the English pottery from miniature sample items he brought with him from England. Turn around time from the time of order to the time of delivery was around one year and a 10% deposit was required. Not a lot known until the 1880s when he was working for Luke Adams pottery in Christchurch as a potter. He died in 1901 or 02. Two complete dinner sets in miniature were carried with George from England. Some items were recovered in Kaikoura a few years ago. Some were purchased in Blenhiem recently and others turned up in an auction recently. The items located in Kaikoura are now in the possession of descendants of Greathead. The other items, including those recently sold on eBay, have been traded by antique dealers. In total around 70-80 pieces of the two sets, originally totaling in excess of 200 items, are known to have survived." $600-800.

    Tree and well meat dish 5" by 3.5",
    Sauce boat, covered vegetable dish,
    Pie dish, salad bowl,
    Tureen with lid and underplate ,
    Large underplate for tureen,
    Various size platters 2.5", 3", 4" wide,
    Large plate and soup bowl 4.25" diameter,
    Smaller plate 3.5" diameter,
    Cheese plate almost 3" diameter.

"EDGE MALKIN & CO" is impressed on this set along with the printed mark "E.M & Co." Below that is the letter "B" and the pattern name "WILLOW." They were located at Newport and Middleport Potteries, Burslem, and used this printed mark from 1873 to 1903. The set is nicely potted and decorated with a brown Willow transfer. We usually think of blue willow but colors of brown, red, or black were also used. This is a nice big set with sixty-three pieces. $1500-1800.

    Soup tureen, underplate, ladle 5.12" high,
    Two sauce tureens, underplate, ladle, 3.75" high,
    Two open vegetables, two pie dishes,
    Butter boat, two pickle dishes,
    Two pie dishes 3.12" long,
    Three meat dishes 3.5" to 5.12" long,
    Six soup dishes 4" diameter,
    Twelve dinner plates 4" diameter,
    Twelve smaller plates 3" diameter,
    Six pastry plates 2.65" diameter,
    Six cheese plates 2.12" diameter.

"T. C. Brown-Westhead Moore & Co." is the impressed trademark. This Staffordshire pottery was located in Hanley. They began using this impressed mark in 1862. This company made tea sets and it is interesting to note that they also made dinner sets. This large set of fifty-five pieces is decorated with light blue transfers in a "Greek Key" pattern. $900-1200.

    Soup tureen, cover, stand and ladle 5" high,
    Two sauce tureens, stands, and ladles 3" high,
    Two covered vegetables, butter boat,
    Salad bowl, two pie dishes,
    Two pickle dishes,
    Five meat dishes 4.25" to 6.5",
    Twelve dinner plates 3.75" diameter,
    Six soup plates 3.75" diameter,
    Six pastry plates 3.12" diameter,
    Six cheese plates 2.62" diameter.

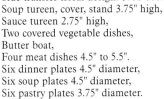

The impressed mark on this dinner service is "Best, P & B." This stands for the company Powell & Bishop, Stafford St. Works, Hanley. They were in business under this partnership from 1876 to 1878. Powell and Bishop date from 1876-1878. Powell, Bishop & Stonier date from 1878-1891. Bishop and Stonier date from 1891 to 1939. This dinner set is earthenware decorated with red line trim and accents. $700-800.

Large tureen with base and ladle 5.25" high,
Small sauce tureen with underplate 3.75" high,
Covered vegetable dish 3.25" high,
Pie dish 3.25" by 4.25",
Butter boat 1.5" high
Three meat dishes (platters) 3.25" by 4.25", to 4.5" by 5.5",
Six plates and three soup plates all 4.5" diameter,
Two pastry plates 3.5" diameter,
One cheese plate 3" diameter.

On this set, the trademark for Bishop & Stonier includes the pattern name "MONTAGUE BORDER." Bishop Stonier was a Staffordshire pottery located in Hanley from 1891 to 1939. The tureen is especially large compared to other dinner sets. It is decorated with a light blue transfer floral design. $700-800.

Soup tureen, cover, stand 3.75" high,
Sauce tureen 2.75" high,
Two covered vegetable dishes,
Butter boat,
Four meat dishes 4.5" to 5.5".
Six dinner plates 4.5" diameter,
Six soup plates 4.5" diameter,
Six pastry plates 3.75" diameter.

"BEST, P&B" is the trademark for the Powell & Bishop Company located in Hanley. It is earthenware decorated with a blue stylized border. Gold trim completes the decorating. This is a large set with serving for six people. $800-1200.

Two small tureens, underplates, and ladle 4" high,
Two covered vegetable dishes,
Salad bowl,
Two butter boats,
Two pie dishes 3.5" by 4.5",
Six meat dishes 3.25" by 4.25" to 4.5" by 5.5",
Six dinner plates 4.5" diameter,
Six pastry plates 3.5" diameter,
Six cheese plates 2.75" diameter.

"P. & B. BEST" is the impressed trademark on this set. This stands for Powell & Bishop from Hanley, England, between 1876 and 1878. On this earthenware set is relief decoration around the handles and finials. It is decorated with a green band with white figures. The soup tureen lid had a hole for the handle of the ladle. This is an extensive set that still contains 52 pieces. $700-800.

Soup tureen with cover and stand 5.87" high,
Two sauce tureens with covers and stands,
Two covered vegetables dishes,
Salad boat, gravy boat, two pie dishes,
Six graduating meat dishes (platters),
Eleven dinner plates 4.5" diameter,
Six soup plates 4.5" diameter,
Six pastry plates 3.5" diameter,
Six cheese plates 3" diameter.

This is a large dinner set with fifty-two pieces. It is earthenware decorated with a green stylized transfer pattern. The center has white stars and designs around a circle with the same theme in the border. The mark on the pieces is a "G" but there is not enough information to identify the manufacturer. $800-1000.

    Covered soup tureen 4" high,
    Underplate for tureen 5.12" long,
    Sauce tureen, underplate and ladle,
    Extra underplate,
    Covered vegetable dish,
    Open serving dish, salad bowl,
    Two pie dishes, butter boat,
    Five platters 4.12" to 5.5" long,
    Two pickle dishes,
    Six soup plates 3.75" diameter,
    Twelve dinner plates 3.75" diameter,
    Six pastry plates 3.12" diameter,
    Six cheese plates 2.6" diameter.

This dinner set was made by Thomas Dimmock & Co. This Staffordshire pottery company was in business from 1828 to 1859. It is interesting to see this dinner set because they made many more tea sets. The set is decorated with a blue ivy vine and blue rims. The two pieces with handles, center-left and bottom-right, are the underplates for the tureens. $700-800.

    One covered vegetable dish with cover,
    Two butter boats,
    Lid to a sauce tureen,
    Two underplates 3" by 4.25" and 3.5" by 5.5",
    Pie dish 3.5" by 4.5",
    Three meat dishes 3.5" by 4.5" to 4.25" by 5.12",
    Six dinner plates and six soup plates 4" diameter,
    Five pastry plates 3.5" diameter.

Early on, English potteries produced some sets with no trademark, which makes it hard for us to identify a manufacturer from more than one hundred and fifty years ago. This set includes thirty-five pieces and is decorated with burgundy bands and line trim. It would date late 1800s. $700-900.

    Tureen, underplate, ladle 4" high,
    Sauce tureen, underplate, ladle 3" high,
    Covered vegetable, open vegetable,
    Pie dish, butter boat,
    Four meat dishes 4.5" to 6" long,
    Six soup plates 3.87" diameter,
    Six dinner plates 3.87" diameter,
    Six plates 3.35" diameter.

This English bone china set is beautifully decorated with blue ribbons and rose-colored flowers. It was purchased in England and the dealer thought it might be a Minton set dating about 1850. $700-900.

    Two covered serving dishes 2.75" high,
    Two platters 4" by 5.25" and 4.5" by 6",
    Sauce pitcher, two small dishes,
    Four plates 4.25" diameter,
    Four plates 3.5" diameter,
    Four plates 3" diameter.

On this set, "MADE IN ENGLAND" is printed in a circle mark. The type of earthenware that shows some crazing and the finials on the covered serving dishes would date the set about the 1920s. It is decorated with decals of exotic colorful birds. The border features colorful flowers. Gold trim completes the decorations. $300-500.

    Two covered serving dishes 3" high,
    Butter boat,
    Three platters 5.75" to 7" long,
    Six plates 5.12" diameter,
    Six plates 4.5" diameter.

"COPELAND, LATE SPODE, ENGLAND" is on the trademark. This factory was located at Stoke-on-Trent, England. This mark was used from 1894 to 1910. The animals pictured are both wild and domestic. This dinner set has a matched tea set. $400-600.

    Large tureen 4.25" high,
    Two small tureens 3.25" high,
    Two covered vegetable dishes 2.25" high,
    Two pie dishes 3.25" by 4.75",
    Four small meat dishes 3.25" by 5",
    Two large meat dishes 3.75" by 5.75" and 4" by 6",
    Two butter or sauce pitchers,
    Small open pedestal dish 3" top diameter,
    Six plates and six soup plates 3.75" diameter
    Six small plates 3.5" diameter.

"Engraved 1832 for W. Ridgway & Co., Semi-china, England" is printed on the base of these pieces. William Ridgway, Son & Co. was located in Hanley. The set would date between 1830 and 1848. This is an outstanding set of the Willow pattern, all hand-painted. The colors are bold with cobalt, burnt orange, rust, and greens. It is unusual to find both the tea set and dinner set in the same pattern. $1500-1800.

    Teapot 5" high,
    Creamer and sugar bowl,
    Four cups and four saucers,
    Four plates 4.25" diameter,
    Four plates 3.87" diameter,
    Two covered serving dishes 3.25" high,
    Sauce pitcher,
    Three platters 4" by 5", 4.75" by 6", and 5.75" by 7.25".

"GOLDEN SWIRL, ENOCH WEDGWOOD (TUNSTALL) LTD. ENGLAND" is the marking on this dinner set. It is from a Staffordshire pottery dating about the middle of the twentieth century. The set is white, decorated with gold bands and trim. $300-400.

    Covered serving dish 3.65" high,
    Butter boat,
    Meat dish 5.5" long,
    Round and square serving dishes,
    Six plates 4.4" diameter.

This dinner set is trademarked "SHELL WARE, ENGLAND." It matches nursery rhyme tea sets featured in this book. It would date from about the 1920s. The sayings are on the front of the pieces. $300-400.
"Mary Had A Little Lamb, Its Fleece As White As Snow"
"There Was An Old Woman Who Lived In A Shoe"
"Ride A Cock Horse To Banbury Cross"
"Tom, Tom The Pipers Son, Stole A Pig And Away He Run"
"Little Jack Horner Sat In A Corner"
"Humpty Dumpty Had A Great Fall"

Two covered serving dishes,
Sauce pitcher,
Platters 4.25" by 5.75" and 5 by 6.5",
Large platter 5.75" by 7",
Six plates 5.25",
Six plates 4.5".

This English dessert service is unmarked but has the same shapes used by Samuel Keeling & Co. in Hanley, between 1840 and 1850. It has brown transfers with polychrome over painting. The decoration is a vase with a floral arrangement giving it an oriental look. The colors are rust, green, teal and yellow. $700-900.
Compote 3.25" high,
Serving piece 3.5" by 5",
Serving piece 4" square,
Serving piece 4" round by 4.5" at the handles,
Six plates 4" diameter.

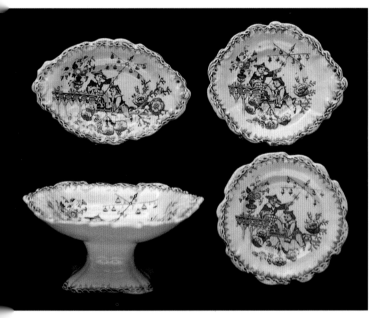

This dessert set is believed to have been made by Charles Meigh, a Staffordshire pottery dating 1835 to 1849. There is an impressed "Stone China" plus "Indian" and another unidentifiable name on the pieces' base. Charles Meigh used this "Chinese Bells" pattern on dinner sets. The dessert set has unique molds. The transfer color is dark green with hand-painted colors in lighter green, red and blue. The base of the compote is rectangle. $600-800.
Compote 2.5" high,
Two oblong serving dishes 5" long,
Oval serving dish 4.25" long,
Eight individual plates 3.87" diameter.

Dessert services are special because they are not as plentiful as tea or dinner services. This set is impressed "BB" for "best body" by the Minton Pottery circa 1860s. The decoration is a version of the "Indian Tree" oriental pattern, which was first designed by Coalport in 1801. It is a beautiful set in bright colors, signed with the decorator's number A238W. $900-1100.
Compote 3" high, top 4.75" by 6.5",
Two oval serving dishes 4" by 5.25",
Two rectangle dishes 4" by 5",
Seven plates 4.75" diameter.

This English dessert service is a little smaller than the average set. It is impressed "OPAQUE PORCELAIN" but no manufacturer is given. There is embossing on all the pieces with little heads on each handle. All the pieces have scalloped edges. It is decorated with red and blue trim. $600-800.

    Compote 2.5" high,
    Two oval serving pieces 4.87" wide,
    Two rectangle serving pieces 4.75" wide,
    Two shell serving pieces 4.25" wide,
    Twelve plates 3.75" diameter.

"RIDGWAYS, ROYAL SEMI PORCELAIN, ENGLAND, HYDE" is the trademark on this dessert set. It is not a full service, but is interesting because Ridgway also made a tea service and dinner service in this same pattern. It would date about the 1880s. $250-350.

    Two compotes 4.6" by 1.12" high,
    Ten plates 4.5" diameter.

This English Staffordshire dessert set is in the shape of a flower. The center is yellow with gold trim. There is an impressed mark but it is not readable. $250-350.

    Compote 2.75" high by 4.25" diameter,
    Four plates 4" diameter.

This dessert server is 12" high. It is a plated rack designed to hold 3 plates. It could be for pies, cakes, cookies, or bars to serve your guest. The plates that came with this server are not very old. The back stamp reads "Registered Trade Mark, A D & Z, from A to Z, Grafton China." They are five inches square. Any plates could be used with this rack. $85-115.

"Crown Staffordshire, England" is on the trademark, dating this piece after 1906. The pattern name is "Ye Olde Willow." This bone china piece is for flower arrangements or pot-pourri, a French name meaning a mixture of flowers, herbs, and spices to create a scent. It has hand-painted details over an outline transfer. $50-75.
Vessel 1.62" by 3.5".

This English syrup pitcher with a pewter top is quite unique. It is decorated with a red sheet pattern. The pewter top has a thumb rest to open the pitcher. It would date around 1880s. $200-300.
Syrup jug 3.75" high to top of thumb rest.

A pair of "Royal Doulton" vases are an interesting accessory to add to a play setting. They have an impressed mark dating them in the early twentieth century. Pair $50-100.
Two vases 3.75" high.

Warming dishes are rare to find. This earthenware dish is set in a metal warming holder with two handles. There is a little chain that holds the cap for the hot water spout. The center is decorated with little pink flowers and green leaves. $400-500.
Warming dish 3.5" diameter.

These are small ceramic plates with ceramic food to use with play settings. These three plates have a pink luster band with center food. They are 2.25" in diameter. They appear to have come from the Staffordshire district in England around 1875 to 1900. They are not quality pieces but interesting to use with the dishes. There are other ceramic food pieces three to four inches in diameter. Each $75-125.

"ENGLAND" is the only marking on this dresser set. It is decorated with a band of stylized flowers and green trim. It is a perfect size to use on a little child's play dresser. $250-350.

Tray 5" by 6.25",
Two candlesticks 3.12" high,
Covered dish 1.75" high,
Ring tree 1.25" high.

English dresser sets are not as common as tea or dinner sets. The set is trademarked "Gemma" with a crown and banner. Below the crest on the front of the pieces is "IN DEO FIDEMUS" and below that is "BRIGHTON." Most of the Crest wares date early twentieth century. $200-300.

    Tray 4" by 6" plus the handles,
    Two candle sticks 2.5" high,
    Tall covered jar 1.25" high,
    Two small covered jars .75" high,
    Ring tree 1" high.

A properly dressed teapot has a little porcelain flower with a cotton roll attached to absorb the drip from the teapot spout.

The hand-made handle holder with lace and ribbons had a little paper note attached: "Put me on your tea pot handle and I will keep your hand from getting to warm." This is on an adult teapot but it is something to watch for in child size.

A shaving mug in this small size is unusual. It is marked "Swan China, England." The front decal has a banner reading "I take But I Surrender" and below that is "Sydney." It is bone china. The upper pierced part is for the soap, the lower part is to dip the brush in water. The size is 2.25 inches high. $25-35.

Finland

The Arabia porcelain factory is located in a suburb of Helsinki, Finland. Arabia was founded in 1874 by the Swedish company, Rorstrand, and in 1916, began as a cooperative. They made table and decorative wares in standard European style. Transfer prints were supplied by the Swedish company, Rorstrand.

"ARABIA, MADE IN FINLAND" is printed on the back stamp. The design of the mark dates the teapot between 1932 and 1949. The teapot is earthenware decorated with red and blue flowers, a little green trim on the handle, finial, base, and leaves. It has a yellow band on the cover. The teapot with the cover is 4" high. There is a matching coffee pot, creamer and sugar bowl, cups and saucers, $20-30.

France

The most notable characteristic of early French porcelain is the pure white color. There were quite a number of porcelain factories around Paris from the late 1700s and all through the 1800s. These wares are also referred to as Old Paris china and are seldom marked. They had fine clays and the factories could produce quality wares. The majority of toy sets date from about the middle of the 1800s. In the late 1800s and into the 1900s French makers produced a wide range of sets using material from pure white porcelain to *faience* (pottery). The wares range from beautifully crafted porcelain to inexpensive toy dishes.

Limoges is a city in France known for its porcelain factories. Limoges wares were white porcelain, usually sold as white ware to be decorated elsewhere. Quite often a mark will include "Limoges, France" and another mark would be the decorator. This is a standard practice and is still common today.

Other well-known names associated with toy dishes include Sarreguemines, Luneville, and Choisy LeRoi.

French hard paste porcelain is nonporous. The body is fired at a high temperature, then glaze is applied and fired at a still higher temperature. This procedure fuses the glaze into the body to create a delicate looking translucent porcelain. The spoilage in this method is higher than glazed pottery thus making it more expensive to make.

In France, earthenwares or semi-porcelain are referred to as half porcelain. Besides the range of materials, there is a wide variation in the shapes and sizes due to the numerous china producing companies. Sizes range from small doll dishes to large services for little girls to use while eating a meal. Another French custom is a display packaging, including items such as table flatware, glassware, and napkins to use in conjunction with the packaged tea service or dinner service. Most of the tureens do not have a cutout in the lid for the handle of the soup ladle. The packaging in wooden display boxes was common before World War I in 1914. After the war, the boxes were usually cardboard.

This French porcelain tea set has the most unusual squat oval shapes. It is fine porcelain decorated with hand-painted birds, possibly a crane, and heavy gold trim. It would date in the last quarter of the nineteenth century. $500-700.

Teapot 2.5" high, Creamer and sugar bowl, Two cups and saucers 3.37" diameter.

This most unusual French set has animal spouts, a dog, and a small figure of a child for the finials. It is white porcelain decorated with gold rims. Another unusual feature is the footed serving pieces. It would date about 1880s. $250-350.

    Teapot 4" high,
    Sugar bowl 3.37" high,
    Six cups and saucers 3" diameter.

This early fine quality French set would date about the 1880s. It is white porcelain with embossed flowers. It is hand-painted over the embossing with blue flowers and green leaves. $400-500.

    Teapot 5.5" high,
    Creamer and sugar bowl,
    Open bowl for sugar lumps,
    Serving tray with handles 6" diameter,
    Four plates 3.75" diameter,
    Four cups and saucers 3.5" diameter.

This French porcelain tea set is decorated with a luster band and gold trim. The handles and finials are black. It is heavy porcelain in a standard French shape dating late 1800s. $400-500.

Teapot 3.25" high,
Creamer and sugar bowl,
Six plates 4" diameter,
Six cups and saucers 3.5" diameter.

This very white porcelain set is decorated with a floral design in pink and gray. The porcelain is thick with interesting molds. Gold trim completes the decoration. Marples identify this as an R.S. Prussia milk can shape, dating before 1903-04. $400-500.

Teapot 5.5" high,
Creamer and sugar bowl,
Four cups and saucers 4" diameter.

French manufacturers produced some very fine porcelain tea sets. All the decorations on this set are silver. The set came in the original box and is complete. $400-600.

Teapot 4" high,
Creamer 2.5" high,
Sugar bowl 2.25" high,
Six plates 3" diameter,
Six cups and saucers 2.5" diameter.

This French porcelain tea set is hand-painted with little flowers and gold trim. The bases of the serving pieces have thick porcelain dating about 1880s. $500-600.

Teapot 5.25" high,
Creamer and sugar bowl,
Four cups and saucers 4.75" diameter.

"L. J. & Cie, FRANCE" is impressed on the base of the pieces. This is an interesting set in both the shapes and the decoration. It has pink roses and gray leaves with dark pink trim dating early 1900s. $400-500.
>Teapot 5" high,
>Creamer and sugar bowl,
>Serving tray 3.75" by 8.25".

This set has the qualities of 1890s French wares. It is a small-sized tea set. It is decorated with a caramel luster band, hand painted floral center in green, blue, and violet. The trim is orange. $200-300.
>Teapot 4.5" high,
>Creamer and sugar bowl,
>Six plates 3.75" diameter,
>Six cups and saucers 3.5" diameter.

This set is unmarked but can be attributed to French manufacturing with its pure white porcelain, the embossed molding on the pieces and the nicely molded handles with a little embossed flower. It is decorated with blue flowers, brown stems and leaves. Gold trim completes the decoration, giving the set an elegant look. $350-500.
>Teapot 6" high,
>Creamer 3.12" high,
>Sugar bowl,
>Two cake plates 4.5" diameter,
>Six cups and saucers 3.35" diameter.

This small set is made of very white porcelain, with fine hand-painted flowers and gold trim. These features and the shapes make it look like it belongs in the French section. This set is not trademarked. It would date between 1890 and 1914. $175-250.
>Teapot 2.75" high,
>Creamer and sugar bowl,
>Four cups and saucers 3.5" diameter.

This small French porcelain tea and dinner service set is doll size. It is nicely decorated with pink bands and little hand-painted flowers. $200-300.
  Teapot 3.5" high,
  Creamer and sugar bowl,
  Six cups and saucers 2.5" diameter,
  Covered serving dish 2.75" high,
  Two platters 2" by 3",
  Sauce pitcher, Double dish,
  Six plates 2.25" diameter.

Dishes marked "Haviland, France" were often made as white ware then sold to other companies to be decorated. The second mark is "Haviland & Co., Limoges, For Burbank Douglass & Co." It is a larger set in fine quality porcelain with exquisite molds and is beautifully decorated. Haviland Company said they never made children's dishes, so this is most likely a demitasse set. $300-500.
  Teapot 5.87" diameter,
  Creamer and sugar bowl,
  Four cups and saucers 4.25" diameter.

This French tea set has a matching dinner set, both made around 1895. The maker is Creil, and this factory existed from 1796 until 1895 in Paris, France. The earthenware is yellowish with a lot of crazing in the glaze. The sugar bowl has a raised ornament on each side in place of the handles. Its decorations are branches with leaves and flowers, all in green. $300-400.
  Teapot 5.87" high,
  Creamer and sugar bowl (missing cover),
  Five cups and six saucers 3.5" diameter.

This is the matching junior size dinner set to the previous tea set. It was made by Creil in Paris, France, in yellowish earthenware dating about 1895. The green transfers are leaves and flowers. Only one vegetable dish belongs to this set. That's normal for French junior sets. $700-900.
  Covered soup tureen with stand 6.87" high,
  Covered vegetable dish,
  Gravy boat with attached underplate,
  Meat platter, salad bowl, pickle dish,
  Fruit dish on high stand,
  Two fruit dishes on low stand,
  Six dinner plates 6.75" diameter,
  Five soup plates 6.76" diameter,
  Four dessert plates 5.5" diameter.

This is a Tête-à-Tête set, meaning a tea service for two persons. It is unmarked but has the same decoration as a set made by "PILIVITE, PORCELAINES DE FEU, PILLIVUYT CIE, MEHUN, MADE IN FRANCE." It is nice quality white porcelain dating 1930s to 1940s. The shapes are graceful with extra gold trim. $150-250.
> Tray 6.75" by 9",
> Teapot with lid 4.75" high,
> Creamer and covered sugar bowl,
> Two cups and saucers 3.25" diameter.

"PORCELAINE OPAQUE, GIEN, FRANCE" is on the trademark. The company established a factory in 1864. Children's sets came from this factory at about the turn of the twentieth century. The transfers are blue with scenes from the story of Little Red Riding Hood. $400-600. The French captions read:
> "Que vous avez de gdes oreilles," meaning what big ears you have.
> "Prends ce chemin," meaning take this path.
> "Porte-lui cette galette," meaning bring her this tart.
> "Je vais voir gd mamam," meaning I'm going to see Grandma.
> Tray 8.25" by 10.25",
> Teapot 3.25" high,
> Creamer and covered sugar bowl,
> Six cups and saucers 2.75" diameter.

French companies produced a large number of play dishes only decorated with gold trim. The porcelain dinner set has a gold band worn on some of the pieces. The set came in a box that was made for Marshall Fields. The tea set is smaller in scale than the dinner set. The porcelain tea set mold is typical of French wares. It is decorated with gold trim. $300-500.
> Tureen and lid 3" high,
> Smaller tureen 2.25" high,
> Butter boat, condiment dish,
> Two platters 4.5" long, compote,
> Eleven plates 3" diameter,
> Six soup plates 3" diameter,
> Teapot 1.75" high,
> Creamer and sugar bowl,
> Six cups and saucers 2" diameter.

This set is trademarked "L.S. & S., Limoges, France" for Siegel & Sohm, dating between 1906 and 1923. French companies made children's play dishes from fine white porcelain. This set has simple lines with gold trim for an elegant looking set. $350-450.
> Teapot 4.25" high,
> Creamer and open sugar bowl,
> Two cups and saucers 3.5" diameter,
> Tray 9.5" by 6.75".

This French dinner service is fine quality and very attractive dating about the 1880s. It came in the original box with horsehair and straw packing material. The set is complete with 42 pieces. The outer rim is gold with a smaller gold line, three black lines and another gold line with a gold line in the center. The edges all have six indents for decoration. Two serving plates have a center hand-painted floral bouquet. $800-1000.

   Soup tureen and lid 4.75" high,
   Two covered serving dishes in metal holders,
   Covered vegetable dish,
   Three meat dishes 3", 4.5", and 5" long,
   Two dishes, 2 and 3 compartments,
   Two mustard and double condiment dishes,
   Three serving dishes,
   Six plates 4" diameter,
   Six soup plates 4" diameter,
   Six smaller plates 3" diameter,
   Six small plates 2.5" diameter.

French companies produced some of the finest porcelain play dishes. This set is a very white porcelain with gold trim, also called Old Paris. It would date about 1870-1880. There are two finials on the tureen and covered dish. It is an especially nice quality dinner set. $800-$1000.

   Large tureen 5" tall,
   Large underplate or service plate 5.6" diameter,
   Covered serving dish 4.75" high,
   Small tureen with attached base 3" high,
   Gravy or butter boat with attached base,
   Salad bowl 4.5" top diameter,
   Two small diamond-shaped dishes 2.5" by 4.5",
   Small meat dish 3" by 4.5",
   Larger meat dish 3.75" by 5.75",
   Four low pedestal dishes 3.8" diameter,
   Eight dinner plates 5" diameter.

This French porcelain dinner set is beautifully made. There is exceptional molding on some of the serving pieces. It is thinly potted with gold rims, lines, stems, and leaves. It has little hand-painted flowers in pink and blue with green leaves. $600-800.

   Soup tureen 3.25" high,
   Sauce tureen with attached underplate 2.75" high,
   Two platters 6" and 7" long,
   Four serving dishes, four compotes,
   Open sauce with attached underplate 2" high,
   Eight plates 3.5" diameter.

This French dinner service is decorated with decals of fruits, nuts and birds. The color is dark teal. The set came packaged with four blue colored glasses 1.75 inches high, two carafes 4.5 inches high and two salt dips. Also included are napkins with holders, flatware with wooden handles and knife rests. $700-800.

   Covered tureen 3.75" high,
   Footed compote 2.25" high by 3.5" top diameter,
   Serving plate 4.5" diameter,
   Platter 3" by 4.25",
   Ridged serving bowl 3.25" diameter.
   Eight plates and eight soup plates all 3" diameter.

"MEDAILLES D'OR, FAIENCERIE DE GIEN, DIPLOMES
D'HONNEUR, PAYSAGES" is the information on the trademark of this
French dinner service. It is a quality set with fine glazing. The blue transfer
is a floral design with a building and a bird on each piece. $700-900.

    Compote 2.5" high by 4.25" top diameter,
    Serving bowl 4" top diameter,
    Serving plate 5" diameter,
    Little double dish,
    Platter 4.62" by 7",
    Six dinner plates 4.25" diameter
    Six soup plates 4.25" diameter,
    Six smaller plates 3.75" diameter

This French dinner set is white, decorated with blue flowers. French dinner
wares included some unusual serving pieces, such as small divided dishes
with two or three sections. Overall the set is unusual in its shapes and
decorations. $700-900.

    Soup tureen 5.75" high,
    Butter boat,
    Platter (meat dish) 5.6" long,
    Six miscellaneous serving dishes,
    Four tiny salt dips,
    Four plates 4" diameter,
    Six plates 3" diameter,
    Four soup plates 4" diameter.

"H. COUDERT, 16 Rue Du Paradis, Paris" is on the trademark of this
dinner service set. It is a very nice set with extremely white earthenware
and smooth glaze. It is decorated with blue transfers that includes many
scenes of children at work and play. There are twelve plates, which would
have been used for two courses of six each. $700-900.

    Large open bowl 2.25" high by 5" diameter,
    Covered serving bowl 3.5" high,
    Sauce boat, small oval dish,
    Serving dish 5.75" diameter,
    Twelve plates 4.37" diameter,
    Six soup bowls, 4" diameter.

This French dinner service is soft paste earthenware decorated with
brown transfers. The border is a garland of flowers. The style would
date the set around 1900. $500-700.

    Large tureen 5" high,
    Smaller tureen 3.75" high,
    Sauce boat and pickle dish,
    Compote 2.5" high,
    Platter 4.25" by 6.25",
    Two serving plates,
    Six plates 4" diameter.

This French porcelain dinner set is decorated with hand-painted enamel flowers. There is gold trim on the embossing and on the rims. The finial is a flower bud. $300-400.

    Soup tureen 4.12" high,
    Sauce tureen 3.37" high,
    Covered vegetable dish,
    Butter boat, pie dish,
    Two meat dishes 3.5" & 4.37" long,
    Six dinner plates 3.37" diameter,
    Six soup plates 3.5" diameter,
    Six pastry plates 2.25" diameter.

This porcelain dinner set is probably French. The set is not marked but the shapes, especially the gravy boat, make it look more like French wares than German wares. It is nicely decorated with gold trim and little roses with little green leaves. The type of porcelain and decoration would most likely date this set about the late 1800s. $700-900.

    Small covered tureen 3.25" high,
    Covered vegetable 3.5" high,
    Compote 2" high by 3.75" diameter,
    Gravy boat, oblong serving dish 4.5" by 8",
    Two small oblong serving dishes 3.75" by 6",
    Six plates 4.5" diameter,
    Six soup plates 4.5" diameter,
    Six smaller plates 4" diameter.

French companies made some of the nicest porcelain play dishes available. This is a nice hard paste porcelain decorated with beige bands with orange and blue lines around the band. This would be a set for six: twelve dinner plates would have been used for two dinner courses. $700-900.

    Large tureen 5.25" high,
    Covered vegetable dish 5.25" diameter,
    Sauce boat, double condiment dish,
    Platter 4.5" by 6.5",
    Two small octagon dishes 4.5" across,
    Deep octagon dish 5.25" across,
    One large plate 6" diameter,
    Six soup bowls 5" diameter,
    Twelve dinner plates 5" diameter.

French pheasants or wild fowl are used to decorate this dinner set. They are decals of large birds possibly pheasants. Each piece features two to four birds. The edges have gold trim. $300-400.

    Two tureens 2.5" high,
    Two butter boats,
    Three platters
    5.25" to 5.87" long,
    Seven plates 4.12" diameter,
    Six plates 3.5" diameter,
    Six plates 3.12" diameter.

French companies have produced some fine sets using fowl as their theme. This set is decorated with a deep red rooster, green base to look like grass, touches of blue and yellow with blue flowers. It is all hand-pained in enamel colors. It is a large bright set with forty-seven pieces. $700-900.

> Two tureens 2.75" high,
> Two covered vegetable dishes,
> Two butter boats with attached bases,
> Two meat dishes 6.25" long,
> Three serving plates 4.32" diameter,
> Four pickle or condiment dishes,
> Two small divided dishes,
> Small covered dish with attached base,
> Tiny pitcher with attached base,
> Four compotes, one compote with bowl top,
> Eleven plates 4" diameter,
> Nine soup plates 4" diameter.

The most interesting feature of this tea set is the way it is packaged. The box has six sides with a deep cover. As the cover lifts off, the bottom flattens out to display the tea set of average quality. The flaps hold the plates and saucers. The center holds the porcelain serving pieces and cups. They are decorated with small hand painted flowers, stems and leaves with gold embellishments. The set includes six napkins and six place cards. $700-900.

> Teapot 3.75" high,
> Creamer and sugar bowl,
> Six plates 3" diameter,
> Six cups and saucers 2.5" diameter.

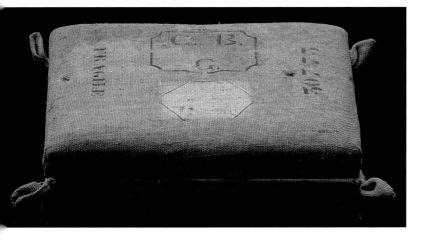

"Dinette" is written in gold letters on the lid of the wooden box that holds this set. This is the French word for children's dinner set and would date from 1925. The box size is 5" high by 13.5" wide by 10.25" deep. The contents are tied to the box with red elastic and blue ribbons. There are relief decorations on the molds. It is decorated with red and blue flowers and gold trim. $600-800.

    Covered vegetable dish 2.5" high,
    Salad bowl, small oval open server,
    Two small meat platters,
    Six dinner plates 3.5" diameter,
    Glass double dish with handles,
    Glass decanter, four wine glasses,
    Glass gravy boat, glass fruit dish,
    Two glass candlesticks, glass basket,
    Four spoons and forks,
    Four linen napkins.

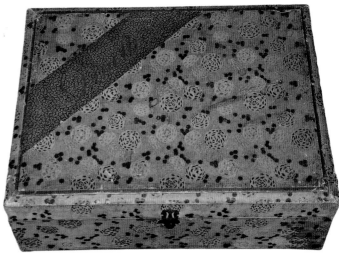

French companies packed their dishes in display boxes more than any other country. The outside of the box is burlap tied at the corners. It would date in the late 1800s. This is an interesting serving set packaged with glassware, tableware, menus, and napkins. It is decorated with deep blue transfers of fruit and birds. It has a twig style border. The glassware is blue. $700-900.

    Soup tureen and lid 3.25" high,
    Covered serving dish,
    Fifteen serving pieces,
    Nine plates 3" diameter,
    Five bowls, five menus,
    Two blue glass carafes 3.75" high,
    Four blue wine glasses, Blue salt dip,
    One soup spoon and four each of knives, forks & spoons.

This French box is in excellent condition with a bright picture of three children on the cover. The white porcelain set is beautifully crafted and decorated with hand-painted flowers and gold trim. The saucers are deep-dish style decorated with hand painted flowers, gold trim, and blue bows. Brass sugar tongs and spoons are added to be ready to serve tea. $500-700.
> Teapot 3.62" high,
> Creamer and sugar bowl,
> Four cups and saucers 4.37" diameter.

"Service de table, Paris" is printed in gold letters on the cover of this wooden box. It measures 5.25" high by 16.5" wide by 11.75" deep. The set includes everything a child would need to serve a meal, all tied to the box with elastic and pink ribbons. This French set is made of good quality porcelain with a lot of relief, dating around 1925. The decal decorations are of children doing different kinds of sports: high jumping, rowing, ice skating, running, playing tennis, boxing, rugby, fencing and riding a bicycle. Flowers and gold rims complete the decorations. $600-800.
> Soup tureen and cover 3.25" high,
> Covered vegetable dish,
> Salad bowl, meat platter, pickle dish,
> Round serving bowl, pedestal fruit dish,
> Gravy boat with attached underplate,
> Four dinner plates and four soup plates 3.5" diameter,
> Glass open salt and pepper dish with handle,
> Glass decanter with cork stopper,
> Four aluminum beakers,
> Four knives, forks and spoons,
> Soup ladle, four napkins.

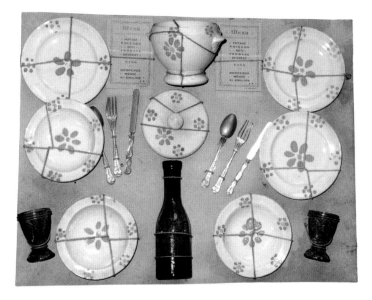

This French set on the original card is missing its box. The earthenware pieces are decorated with green and yellow. It is interesting to have the glassware, flatware, and menus included. $250-350.

Soup tureen with lid 3.5" high,
Three soup bowls 3.25" diameter,
Three plates 3.5" diameter,
Brown carafe, two blue tumblers,
Pewter flatware,
Two menus written in French.

This style French set is called Quimper even thought this set is unmarked. The figures represent the Breton peasants of France. A peasant man is handing a flower to a peasant woman. The background is cream color with hand-painted figures. The border is sponged blue. It would date in the first half of the 1900s. Included is a tea tile. $500-600.

Covered serving bowl,
Tea tile 3.5" diameter,
Large serving plate 4.5" diameter,
Platter 2.75" by 4.25",
Sauce pitcher,
Four plates and four bowls 3" diameter.

Some French company packaged this bright yellow Quimper dinner set with glassware, flatware, menus and napkins. The center is decorated with hand-painted ships. The rims are blue. The flatware is brass with marble-ized celluloid handles and includes four place settings. The glassware includes two decanters and four tumblers. $700-900.

Soup tureen with lid 3.25" high,
Butter boat, trivet,
Two meat dishes 4.25" and 5.62" long,
Serving plate 5" diameter,
Four dinner plates 4" diameter,
Four soup plates 4" diameter.

This French dinner set is deep pink, decorated with a blue sponged edge. It is not marked but was called Quimper. A French factory was located at Loc Maria near Quimper in the 1700s. HB is the modern mark since 1872 copying the 18th century wares that we call Quimper. This set is most likely early 20th century. $500-700.

Tureen and lid 2.75" high,
Butter boat, two serving dishes,
Four bowls 3" diameter,
Two platters 4.37" by 2.87",
Six plates and six soups all 3" diameter.

"Service de Table, PARIS, ELD Marque Déposée" is printed on the cardboard box lid. The china pieces are marked "P. aut. WALT DISNEY, S. A." This dinner set features Mickey Mouse and Minnie Mouse. The set also includes aluminum tumblers, flatware, and napkins for four place settings. $300-400.
  Covered tureen 3.5" high,
  Platter 3.25" by 4.5",
  Four bowls 3" diameter,
  Four plates 3" diameter.

"HB QUIMPER, FRANCE" is printed on the trademark. It is a small sized tête-à-tête set in beige and brown colors. The stylized design is unusual in Quimper wares. $400-600.
  Tray 5.25" diameter,
  Teapot 2" high,
  Creamer and sugar bowl,
  Two cups and saucers 2" diameter.

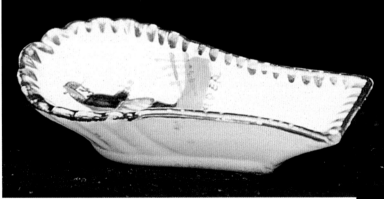

"© W.D.P., M.F.P." is trademarked on the china. The wooden box has "Au Nain Bleu, 06 RUE ST. HONORE, PARIS." The set is nicely packaged in the original box with the serving plate featuring Donald and Daisy Duck. Another plate features Huey, Louie and Dewey, who are Donald's nephews. The other plates include Donald or Daisy Duck. These characters first appeared in 1934. The box size is 18 by 22 inches. Also included in the original box are six glass tumblers, 1.5 inches high, embossed "FRANCE" on the bottom, and six aluminum spoons 3.5 inches long. $400-500.
  One serving plate 7" to the edge of the handles,
  Six individual plates 4.5" diameter.

"HB Quimper" is printed on the front of the little spoon rest. It is decorated with the standard French peasant and cobalt edge trim. $40-75.
  Spoon rest 3.5" long.

Pots De Crème is a rarity in child's play size. The set consists of a porcelain pedestal base with seven base rims to hold the cups. It is seven inches in diameter and two inches high. Each cup is 1.3 inches high, with a 1.5 inch top diameter. With a cover it is two inches high. It is white porcelain with gold rims and gold trim on the finials and handles. $800-1200.

Here is a recipe for "Pots de Crème A la Vanille"

3 cups heavy cream
6 egg yolks
¼ cup sugar
1/8 teaspoon salt
1 ½ teaspoons vanilla extract.

Adjust rack to the center of the oven. Preheat the oven to 350 degrees.

Scald the cream over hot water in the top of a large, uncovered double boiler on moderate heat until tiny bubbles begin around the edge or a slight wrinkled skin forms on top.

Meanwhile, stir the egg yolks with a fork, or very briefly with a wire whisk just to mix them-do not beat any air into them. When the cream is scalded, remove it from the heat, add the sugar and salt, and stir to dissolve. Stirring constantly, very gradually pour the hot cream into the yolks. Do not beat enough to make any foam. Stir in the vanilla and strain into a pitcher.

Pour into ovenproof cups, using either about a dozen pots de crème pots with lids, or seven or eight custard cups. Do not fill them too full. (If you use pots de crème pots, be sure to leave enough headroom so that the lids do not touch the custard.) With a small spoon remove any foam that might have formed.

Place in a baking pan, which must not be deeper than the cups. Pour in hot water to about halfway up the cups. Cover the crème pots with their covers: Place a piece of aluminum foil or a cookie sheet over the tops of the custard cups.

Bake for 25 to 30 minutes or until a small, sharp knife inserted into the custard just barely comes out clean. Remove from hot water and cool uncovered on a rack. When completely cool, the pots de crème pots may be re-covered. Refrigerate covered.

Optional: A spoonful of whipped cream on the top of these seems to cut their richness, unlikely as it sounds. (Either with or without the whipped cream, if you have candied violets or rose petals this is a good time to use them - just one on each.)

Dessert services are special because they are more rare than tea or dinner services. This French set is porcelain with pink bands, black and gold line trim and gold edge trim. There are four different sizes of pedestal dishes, a strawberry dish and twelve individual plates. $900-1200.

One footed strawberry dish 4" diameter,
Large compote 2.5" high by 4.5" top diameter,
Smaller compote 2" high by 3.75" top diameter,
Two large low pedestal dishes
1.75" high by 4.5" top diameter,
Two smaller low pedestal dishes
1.25" high by 4" top diameter,
Twelve individual plates 3.5" diameter.

"FRANCE" with "LIMOGES" in a star is the trademark. This is a beautiful porcelain dessert set decorated with hand-painted flowers, green leaves and stems with a butterfly. $400-500.

Large service plate 6" diameter,
Two small platters 2.25" by 4",
One compote 1.5" high, by 3.5" top diameter,
Sauce boat,
Six plates and six bowls all 3.5" diameter.

This small-sized dessert service was made in France. It is a lovely white porcelain set decorated with a band of hand-painted flowers in pink, blue, red and green. It is trimmed with gold embellishments and rims. $400-500.

Three compotes 1.37" high by 2.75" diameter,
Two berry dishes .62" high by 3.25" diameter,
Two low flat compotes 1" high by 3.25" diameter,
Twelve individual plates 2.75" diameter.

"P L Limoges France" is on the trademark. This dresser set only has two pieces: the tray and hat pin holder. It is decorated with hand-painted flowers and gold trim. $75-125.

Tray 3.25" by 4.5",
Hat pin holder 2" high.

The little enamel plate on the front of this wooden wash stand with a ceramic top says "Sarreguemines, DIGOIN, LAVABO BEBE, Déposé." In 1871, following the annexation of the Moselle area by Germany, two new Sarreguemines factories were constructed at Digoin and Vitry-le-François (both in France). In 1913, the Sarreguemines company (Utzschneider & Cie) was split into two companies one in France and one in Germany. This French set would date circa 1900. On this set, "LAVABO BEBE" means baby wash stand, and "Déposé" means registered. The decals are Kate Greenaway figures. The little pot on the top right doesn't belong with the set, but is a Sarreguemines Kate Greenaway mustard pot. It doesn't come with a lid but with a cork stopper. $1500-2000.

    Wooden stand 19 inches high, by 18" wide, by 14" deep,
Double wash bowl, child size,
Large pitcher for water,
Mustard pot (use for flowers or hat pins),
Small plates for soap and sponge.
Antique towels on the towel bars.

This small doll-size wash stand set is unmarked, but looks like French in both the color of the fine porcelain and the style. The decoration is lavender bands with black line trim. The handle on the pitcher is a dragonhead in gray color. $250-350.

    Pitcher 3.5" high,
Bowl 1.25" high by 3.75" top diameter,
Soap dish 1.75" high by 1.5" wide by 2.5" long,
Powder dish 1.75" high,
Open bowl for the sponge 2.25" diameter.

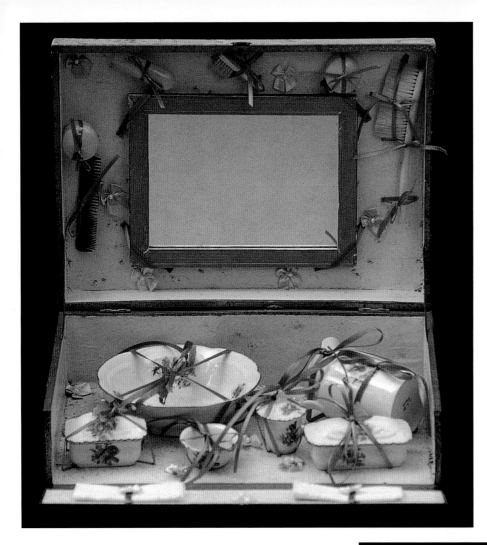

A French company packed this wash stand set in a wooden box, dating it in the late 1800s. The cover of the box has "Service, Faience, C B G, Paris." Inside the cover is a mirror 6.12 by 7.87 inches. The wash stand pieces have nice white porcelain decorated with sprigs of flowers. The little extra pieces are early celluloid. They include three covered boxes, toothbrush holder, hairbrush and comb. Two little towels complete the set. $400-500.

Wash bowl 5.75" diameter,
Pitcher 4.5" high,
Soap holder 2.5" long,
Toothbrush holder 3.5" long,
Small sponge bowl 2" diameter,
Covered cup 1.75" high.

Wash stand sets or chamber sets were packaged with extra items in their original French boxes. The picture on the cover of the box is of two little girls playing with a doll. "AMIDON REMY" is written on the picture. The interesting feature is all the extra small pieces that were included. It has an oriental theme, decorated in burnt orange trim and hand-painted flowers. It has bamboo style handles and finials. It contains twelve porcelain pieces and plus nineteen miscellaneous pieces. $500-600.

Pitcher 3.5" high, bowl 5" diameter,
Soap dish with lid, toothbrush holder with lid,
Sponge dish, small bowl, two covered containers,
Three glass scent bottles, glass jar with lid,
Hairbrush, clothes brush, copper mirror, comb,
Towel, sachet, two soaps, sponge, two scented bars.

Germany

Germany exported large quantities of children's play dishes from the 1870s to the onset of World War 1 in 1914. Prior to this time there were limited numbers of dishes from some of the finest companies such as Meissen. After World War 1 ended in 1918, the factories began rebuilding. Some sets that are trademarked but do not have "Made In Germany" were not intended for export. Many of the earlier sets were not marked at all, and later were usually marked "Germany." Since 1891 the McKinley Tariff Act required that all items imported into the United States have "Made In" country of origin. A few sets included the manufacturer's trademark. Sometimes only one piece in a set was marked.

R. S. Prussia toy china is a whole collection in itself. Some of the 1880s and 1890s sets that are unmarked were thought to be German or French. Thanks to Carol and Leland Marple and their book *R. S. Prussia: The Formative Years* we now know that a majority of these sets were made at the R.S. Prussia Factory. The Marples have done a wonderful job of identifying molds and handles on these German wares and have included a whole chapter on the children's toy sets. Any collector of children's dishes needs this book in their library.

The German occupation held by the American, English, and French created the Federal Republic of Germany on September 21, 1949. In 1952 East Germany announced measures to isolate from West Germany. This led to the construction of the Berlin Wall, which began in August 1961. The wall was torn down in 1989. Dishes or toys marked Federal Republic of Germany (West Germany) would date between 1949 and 1989. Dishes marked German Democratic Republic (East Germany) would date 1952 to 1989.

A majority of the German dishes are porcelain, ranging from very fine to poor quality. The best dishes could include molded relief, fancy handles and finials with beads and embossed scrolls, perfectly placed decals, and quality craftsmanship. The other range is earthenware, poor quality work with flaws and bumps, crooked decals, and uneven shapes using unskilled labor.

Favorite topics for decorating play dishes include scenes of children at play, faces of children, scenes from nursery rhymes, and pictures of various animals. German makers often used gold trim or luster in their decorating. Pink luster was the most common, but shades of blue, green, and yellow were also used.

Some manufacturers produced undecorated white china that was either sold for use as white ware or sold to other companies to be decorated. Decals were made and sold to any company. That is the reason you can find the same decals on dishes from different manufacturers and countries.

Children's sets came packaged in two, four, or six place settings with or without individual plates. Sometimes a serving plate or dish was included. Germany made tea sets, coffee sets, dinner sets, chocolate sets, toilet sets, and miscellaneous specialty sets. Germany served more coffee than tea so it stands to reason that more coffee services were made for children. When little girls had a party it would usually be referred to as a tea party regardless of what beverage was being served.

This wonderful German porcelain set is in the shape of a conch shell. It is colored caramel luster with a lighter luster representing the inside of the shell. It came in the original box with a note on the inside cover: "Nellie Waterbury from Johnnie Ellis, 1862." $700-900.
Teapot 4.25" to shell peak,
Creamer and sugar bowl,
Four cups and saucers 3.12" diameter.

This is an exquisite set in both the molding and the coloring. It is fine quality porcelain with raised porcelain flowers and raised trim on all the pieces. The green coloring is feathered from the edge to the center. The bases of the serving pieces have extra stress porcelain crosses or bars. $1000-1400.

Teapot 4.87" high,
Creamer and covered sugar bowl,
Two serving plates 5" diameter,
Two cups and saucers 4.12" diameter.

R.S. Prussia is credited as having made this set between 1888 and 1894. They also used the same decoration with applied dots on some adult pieces. It is beautifully decorated with rose-colored flowers and blue to yellow leaves, all outlined with gold beading. The porcelain has applied dots giving it a rough look to the background. The quality of this set makes it easy to confuse with French wares, but thanks to the work of Marples this set is identified as R.S. Prussia. $700-900.

Teapot 5.25" high,
Creamer 3.25" high,
Sugar bowl 3.12" high,
Six plates 3.75" diameter,
Six cups and saucers 3.75" diameter

R. S. Prussia made this coffee service in an outstanding beautiful mold and decoration. The tall coffeepot is decorated with tulip flowers. The mold is exceptionally fine with gold trim enhancing the embossing. $2500-3000.

Coffee 6.5" high,
Creamer 2.25" high,
Sugar 3.25" high,
Two plates 6" diameter,
Two cups and saucers 4.25" diameter.

This child's set is finely made with embossing on all the pieces. It is white porcelain with gold trim and pink flowers. The handles and finials are designed to look like coral. It has applied dots on a lovely mold. Unmarked, it was thought to be American Belleek but it is typical of wares that were made by R.S. Prussia in the years 1888 to 1894. $300-400.

Teapot with cover 3.75" high,
Creamer and covered sugar bowl,
One serving plate with handles 4.75" diameter,
Four plates 3.37" diameter,
Four cups and saucers 2.75" diameter.

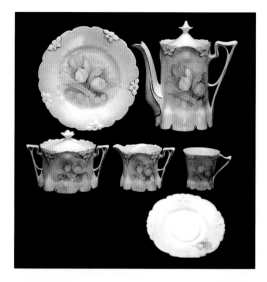

R. S. Prussia is credited as the maker of this tea set. This seems to be their most popular mold for the children's tea sets. It has lovely embossed molds in fine porcelain. The decorations vary from soft floral patterns to bold colors. This set is elegant with light cream color edges and gold trim over grapes decor. The cake plate is outstanding. $1500-1800.

    Teapot 4.75" high,
    Creamer and covered sugar bowl,
    Cake plate 5" diameter,
    Six cups and saucers 3.75" diameter.

R.S. Prussia is credited with this mold. There is a row of embossed beading around the base and on the top. It is decorated with large white flowers, a yellow center and green leaves. There is light blue shading on the tops of the pieces. $1300-1700.

    Teapot 4.75" high,
    Creamer and covered sugar bowl,
    Six cups and saucers 3.75" diameter.

R. S. Prussia is credited with this mold. This set has dark blue border trim with gold floral designs. The center is a series of rose flowers, green leaves and stems. $900-1400.

    Teapot 5" tall,
    Covered sugar bowl,
    Two serving plates 5" diameter,
    Six cups and saucers 3.75" diameter.

R. S. Prussia is the manufacturer of this tea set decorated with red poppy flowers with green leaves and grass. The shading is very light green. Gold trim completes the decorations. $900-1400.

    Teapot 5" high,
    Creamer and sugar bowl,
    Two cups and saucers 4" diameter.

R. S. Prussia is credited as the manufacturer of these serving pieces. It is a smaller set with pink shading around the soft floral design. The flowers are purple and white lilacs. $300-400.
  Teapot 4" high,
  Creamer 2.25" high,
  Sugar bowl 2" high

R.S. Prussia is the maker of the tea set. It is a common mold decorated with pink background and soft flowers. The serving pieces have gold painted over the embossing. The little plates and saucers have ridges. The saucers have gold around the base where the cup would sit. $900-1200.
  Teapot 4" high,
  Creamer and sugar bowl each 2.37" high,
  Six plates 3" diameter,
  Six cups and saucers 3.5" diameter.

This is an R.S. Prussia mold with a peach to light yellow background. A floral design is in the center and gold rims complete the decoration. This coffee set has a matched dinner set. $900-1200.
  Coffee pot 5.62" high,
  Creamer and sugar bowl,
  Six plates 4" diameter,
  Six cups and saucers 3.75" diameter.

R. S. Prussia is using the same mold for these serving pieces as in the previous set. The plates and saucers are from a different mold. This set is decorated in a yellow and green background with a large flower with leaves. The saucer has a scalloped edge. $900-1200.
  Teapot 4" high,
  Creamer and covered sugar bowl,
  Six plates 3" diameter,
  Six cups and saucers 2.75" diameter

This is a beautiful German porcelain coffee service with lovely molding, circa 1910. There is embossing, some of which has been decorated with gold trim. The decals are a soft floral in multicolors. Gold rims complete the decoration. $400-600.
    Coffee pot 5.5" high,
    Creamer 3.12" high,
    Covered sugar bowl 3" high,
    Six plates 4" diameter,
    Six cups and saucers 3.87" diameter.

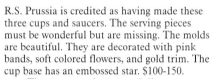

R.S. Prussia is credited as having made these three cups and saucers. The serving pieces must be wonderful but are missing. The molds are beautiful. They are decorated with pink bands, soft colored flowers, and gold trim. The cup base has an embossed star. $100-150.
    Three cups and saucers 4" diameter.

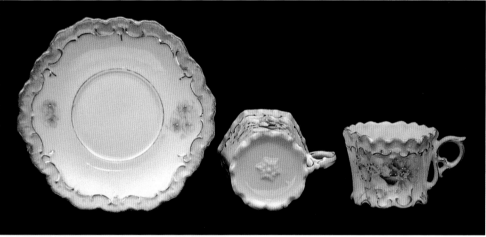

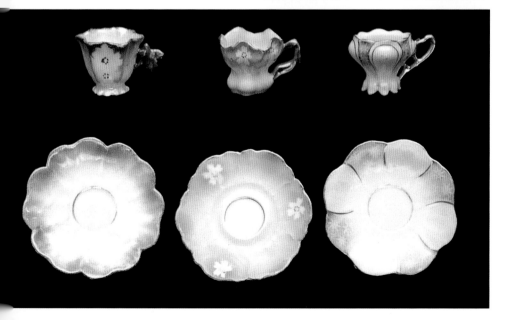

Here are three tiny R. S. Prussia cups and saucers. Each porcelain cup and saucer is a different mold in exquisite craftsmanship. The cups are one inch high with 2.5-inch diameter saucers. Each $150-250.

E.S. Factory stands for Erdmann Schlegelmilch. Erdman's three sons ran the factory and they named it for their father. The factory went through good times and bad times. It finally closed for good in 1935. They manufactured goods mainly for the export market. They used these transfers on some of their wares. This is called the four seasons. It is a woman with a flower crown in her hair. Spring has small flowers, summer has daisies, fall has colorful autumn leaves, and winter has a holly wreath. This is an exquisite German porcelain coffee set. The molds are beautifully molded with embossing on every piece. The edges are all fluted and trimmed with added green floral and leaves. $1500-1800.

 Coffee pot 5.75" high,
 Creamer 3.5" high,
 Sugar bowl 3.75" high,
 Six plates 3.25" diameter,
 Six cups and saucers 4.25" diameter.

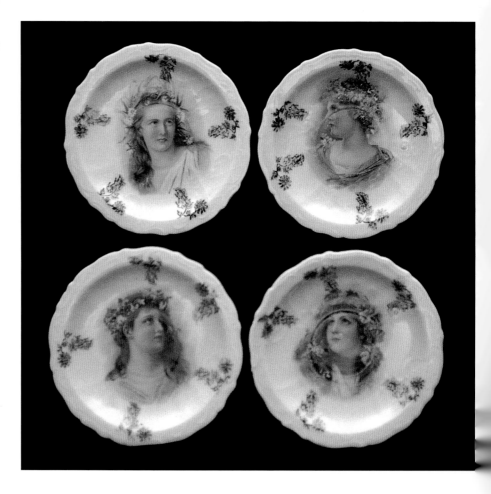

This unmarked German tea or coffee service is credited to the early Reinhold Schlegelmilch factory (R. S. Prussia). It is painted over the glaze and shows some wear. $125-150.

Coffee or tea server 4.75" high,
Creamer 3.25" high,
Sugar bowl 3" high,
Six plates 3.25" diameter,
Six cups and saucers 3" diameter.

This fine porcelain coffee set has a lovely mold shape. The trim is green with floral decorations. The creamer and sugar bowl are small compared to the coffeepot. The cups are a mug shape with ridges and there are ridges on the saucers as well. The plate is smaller with floral decorations. The plate and saucer features are reminiscent of R.S. Prussia sets. $700-900.

Coffee pot 5.12" high,
Creamer 2.5" high,
Sugar bowl 2.12" high,
Six plates 2.6" diameter,
Six cups and five saucers 3.25" diameter.

This German porcelain tea set is not trademarked. The bottoms of the pieces are flat. The flowers are hand-painted, dating the set late 1800s. Embossing and shades of blue complete the decoration. $250-350.

Teapot 4.5" high,
Creamer and sugar bowl,
Six cups and saucers 3.75" diameter.

This set is credited to R.S. Prussia. The set has cobalt trim on all the rims with gold flowers and leaves on each serving piece and cups. The saucers just have the blue rim. $500-700.

Tea or coffee pot 5.25" high,
Creamer 2.5" high,
Covered sugar bowl,
Six cups 1.5" high,
Six saucers 3.25" diameter.

This coffee or cocoa set came in the original box dating late 1800s. It may belong to the Prussia potteries. It is of a lesser quality than later sets. The finish has a rough texture. The serving pot cover has a simple style finial. It has heavy embossing with hand-painted purple flowers and teal colored trim with gold embellishment. The serving pot is large compared to the creamer and sugar bowl. All three serving pieces have three feet. $500-700.

    Coffee pot 6.12" high,
    Creamer 2.6" high,
    Sugar bowl 2.5" high,
    Six plates 2.6" diameter,
    Six cups and saucers 2.6" diameter.

The box for this tea set looks like it would date in the 1880s to early 1900s. The box is printed "MADE IN GERMANY." The tea set is not marked. It is an early crude pottery set with a portrait on the teapot. There are raised medallions with little flowers on each piece. It is decorated with a blue Greek key design, painted pink ribbons and gold trim. $200-300.

    Teapot 5.5" high,
    Creamer and sugar bowl,
    Six plates 4" diameter,
    Six cups and saucers 3.5" diameter.

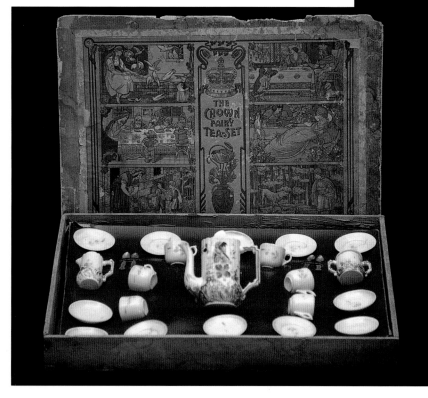

The cover of this set's box reads "THE CROWN FAIRY TEA SET" and the impressed word "Crown" is on the back of the teapot. The set is complete in the original wooden box with the name "Schutz-Marke." It was made by Gebruder Heubach in Lichte, Thuringen, who began using this mark in 1882. It has embossing on the serving pieces, poorly painted with cheap gold paint and flowers. There is a decal of a Gypsy on the teapot. Only the fronts of the pieces are painted. The box cover is the most interesting part of this set with scenes from *Cinderella, Snow White and the Seven Dwarfs, Hansel & Gretel, Puss & Boots, Sleeping Beauty*, and *Little Red Riding Hood*. $150-250.

    Teapot 5" high,
    Creamer and sugar bowl,
    Six plates 2.62" diameter,
    Six cups and saucers 2.62" diameter.

"CM" and "MADE IN GERMANY" are printed on the box. "Gesetzlich geschutzt" is on the cover, which means it is registered. It would date around 1900. The box cover pictures nine girls around a table. On the four corners are pictures of children. It is unusual to have such a tall coffeepot in a child's service. The other pieces are small compared to the coffeepot. The set has lovely shapes decorated with irises and pink trim. Only the fronts are decorated to show in a display box. $200-300.

    Coffee pot 7.37" high,
    Creamer and sugar bowl,
    Six plates 3.5" diameter,
    Six cups and saucers 4" diameter.

This is a heavy German porcelain set dating around 1880s. It has embossed flowers and leaves on the pieces and the finials. There is a little gold trim on the handles and spout. The saucers are very small. $400-500.

    Coffee server 6" high,
    Creamer and sugar bowl,
    Two serving plates 4.5" to edge of handles,
    Six cups and six tiny saucers 2.25" diameter.

    This set came packaged in the same type cardboard box as the previous set and next set. Only the box is marked "Made In Germany" with the logo "CM" intertwined. It has unusual shapes with orange trim. It is interesting to see sets so completely different in the same style box. $200-300.

    Serving pot 5.5" high,
    Creamer and sugar bowl,
    Four cups and saucers 4" diameter.

This porcelain set could be considered for either coffee or cocoa, as it is an in-between size. It has an elegant mold with embossing in fine porcelain. It has soft floral decorations on a blue background. Gold feathering edges add elegance to the set. Many of these features are reminiscent of some of the R. S. Prussia sets. $500-700.
    Coffee pot 5.25" high,
    Creamer and covered sugar bowl,
    Five plates 3.5" diameter,
    Six cups and saucers 3" diameter.

Germany would be the maker of this unmarked coffee set. It could be from the factory of early Reinhold Schlegelmilch (R.S. Prussia), dating around 1890s. It has the taller pot as Germany served more coffee than tea. It is decorated with flowers in orange and purple, green leaves and grass, and gold trim. $300-400.
    Coffee pot 5" high,
    Creamer and sugar bowl,
    Six plates 3.75" diameter,
    Six cups and saucers 3.25" diameter,
    Two cake plates 4.75", and 5.25" to the edges of handles.

Here is another set in fine porcelain with embossing. The covers are dome shape with small finials. The floral decoration is in orange and yellow with moss green leaves. Gold trim completes the decorations. Some of the R. S. Prussia influence is that the plate is smaller than the saucer and the covers feature small finials. $500-700.
    Coffee pot 4.75" high,
    Creamer 2.6" high,
    Sugar bowl 2.4" high,
    Five plates 2.75" diameter,
    Five cups and saucers 2.87" diameter.

Villeroy & Boch from Wallerfangen, Germany, made a lot of nice children's dishes. This coffee service is made of earthenware, circa 1880. This mold was used with different decorations. The transfers include a girl knitting while she's watching a flock of sheep; two deer in a forest; a water mill; a little mountain village with a church tower; and a woman wearing a straw hat with large pompons around the crown, which is the local costume of the Black Forest. $300-400.
    Coffee pot 5.62" high,
    Creamer and covered sugar bowl,
    Two cups and saucers 3.62" diameter.

Villeroy and Boch made these two plates, which came out of a dinner set, about the 1880s. The scenes are cottages. This style is similar to the preceding tea set. Each plate $35-50.

Plates 4.25" diameter.

Schafer & Vater are the porcelain makers of this unusual tea set. They were located in Rudolstadt, Germany. The company was in business from 1890 to 1962. The sugar bowl and cups are in the shapes of faces that are on the front and on the back. The teapot spout is a long nose. The covers have bow finials. The oval saucers are decorated with a flower rim. The serving pieces have earrings for added interest. The colors are pink in a matte finish. $1000-1500.

Teapot height 5.5" high,
Covered sugar bowl 4.5" high,
Creamer 3" high,
Two cups and oval saucers 4.5" by 5".

This German porcelain tea set would date late 1800s. It is fluted on all the pieces. It is decorated with blue and gold trim. $300-400.
    Teapot 3.75" high,
    Creamer and sugar bowl,
    Four plates 5.25" diameter,
    Four cups and saucers 4.25" diameter.

"Rose O'Neill, Kewpie, Germany" is signed on this porcelain tea set. Rose O'Neill was the creator of Kewpies who first appeared in 1909. These dishes date about 1915. This set includes many poses of Kewpies. The luster shading is green-gray and the plate luster has light shades of green, orange and purple. $1000-1400.
    Teapot 5.25" high,
    Creamer 2.5" high,
    Sugar bowl 3.5" high,
    Six plates 5.25" diameter,
    Six cups and saucers 4.5" diameter.

This is the second set of Kewpies in the same mold. The decorations are military figures with hats. The luster edge trim is light green. It is trademarked "Copyrighted Rose O'Neill Wilson, KEWPIE, Germany." Set $1000-1400.

This German tea set would date about 1880s. The most interesting features are the finials shaped as the head of a bird. A gray band and gold trim complete the decoration. $300-400.
    Teapot 5" high,
    Sugar bowl,
    Six cups and saucers 3.75" diameter.

This German tea set has some very nice qualities. It is hand-painted with floral decorations and blue rims. The teapot spout features an animal head. There is a wide lip on the creamer. It has very nice handles and molding. It would date about the 1880s. $300-400.

    Teapot 4" high,

    Creamer and sugar bowl,

    Six cups and saucers 4.75" diameter.

This is the second set by Swaine & Co. It is not trademarked but has the same mold as the previous set dating 1900-1920. The mold has heavy embossing and is decorated with brown scenes of windmills and sailboats. $400-700.

    Teapot 3.25" high,

    Creamer 3" high,

    Covered sugar bowl 2.75" high,

    Four cups and saucers 3.87" diameter.

"GERMANY" with a "D" and crossed pipes are the trademark. It is from Swaine & Co. dating between 1900-1920. They are located in Huttensteinach in Thuringer, Germany. In their advertisement of wares, they also list "Kinderservice," which means children's service. The shapes are especially interesting with heavy molding on all the pieces. The finials are a little bud. The transfer is under the glaze. It represents a cottage by a windmill with foliage and sailboats on the water. The other scenes show a house. It is a quality set. $400-700.

    Teapot 3.5" high,

    Creamer and covered sugar bowl,

    Six plates 3.75" diameter,

    Six cups and saucers 3.85" diameter.

These lovely German serving pieces have unique shapes. The decorations are in the style of Kate Greenaway children. The set has dark green borders. $100-150.

    Teapot 5" high,

    Creamer 3.12" high,

    Open sugar bowl 2" high.

Roosevelt Bears are pictured on this tea set. The name comes from the story that Theodore Roosevelt went on a hunting trip and refused to shoot a bear cub. Seymour Eaton wrote books on the adventures of two bears. They were called Teddy B for the black bear and Teddy G for the gray bear. Manufacturers began making Teddy Bears and other novelty items such as dishes from about 1906. The decals do show some wear. $1200-1500.

  Teapot 5" high,
  Creamer 2.25" high,
  Sugar bowl 2.75" high,
  Four plates 3.25" diameter,
  Four cups and saucers 2.5" diameter.

Royal Bayreuth children's ware would date between 1890 and 1917. Then Royal Bayreuth had a large fire that destroyed most of the molds. This teapot is pictured because it has a different shape than other sets pictured. Its background colors are in the style of Royal Bayreuth. It is decorated in graded colors from blue, green, purple, and pink. The decal is Jack and Jill falling down the hill, spilling a pail of water. $250-350.
    Teapot 4" high.

Robinson Crusoe is the theme on this child's set circa 1910. This is not a fine quality set but it is interesting because of the decals. It is decorated on the front to be shown in a display box. The backs are plain white. There are little painted flowers around the decals. The decals include Robinson Crusoe; a sinking ship; a man running; Robinson by a ladder against a tall fence; a large sailing ship; Robinson sitting at a table with a bird, cat and dog; five goats grazing; Robinson and Friday on the boat. $600-800.

Robinson Crusoe was an Englishman who had a longing for the sea. On a voyage to Africa the ship broke apart on a reef near an island. Robinson was the only one to survive. He constructed a raft and brought food, ammunition, water, wine, clothing, tools, sailcloth and lumber from the broken ship. He made a sailcloth tent on the side of a small hill and built a fence of tall sharp stakes. He enlarged his makeshift home and built furniture. He ate wildfowl and small game. He found several springs for water. He was able to grow corn, barley and rice. He lived this way for the next twenty-four years. He read a Bible every morning and night and thanked God for delivering

him from the sea. Some prisoners paddled over from another island, Robinson shot some and frightened others away. He rescued one man and named him Friday who became his faithful servant and friend. Robinson taught Friday English. A hostile tribe invaded the island and they were no longer safe. An English ship was near shore and they were able to return to England after thirty-five years in June 1687. There Robinson married and had three children. In 1695 Robinson sailed as a private trader to the East Indies and China. On the way to Brazil savages attacked the ship and Friday was killed. From the coast of China Robinson worked his way home to live out the rest of his life. This is a very short version of his adventures.

  Teapot 5.75" high,
  Creamer and covered sugar bowl,
  Six plates 3" diameter,
  Six cups and saucers 3" diameter.

This German porcelain tea set is decorated with holly berries and gold trim. This mold is the same style as the Roosevelt Bears set but is a little smaller. The decoration is over the glaze so there is some wear. The interesting pieces with this set are the open serving bowls and basket with a handle. It will fit into the Christmas section of your collection. $300-400.

    Teapot 4.25" high,
    Creamer 2.25" high,
    Sugar 2.5" high,
    Two open serving dishes,
    Basket 3.25" to top of handle,
    Six cups and saucers 3.25" diameter.

This little German porcelain set had been decorated over the glaze. Most of the decorations have worn off. It has nice shapes in an inexpensive set. $75-125.

    Teapot 2.25" high,
    Creamer and sugar bowl,
    Five plates 3.5" diameter,
    Five cups and saucers 3.25" diameter.

This set shows "S & Y" is on the banner on the trademark but the maker is unknown. The design of the mark is similar to other German marks. It is decorated in blue floral transfers. It has nice molds but need pieces to complete the set. $100-200.

    Teapot 4" high,
    Creamer,
    Plate 4.75" diameter,
    Cup 2" high.

This German porcelain tea set is unusual with the mushroom cap covers. It has a green background that is brighter than the picture shows. It is decorated with decals of flowers and then hand-painted red flowers or dots and green leaves. $400-600.

    Teapot 3.25" high,
    Creamer and covered sugar bowl,
    Four plates 4" diameter,
    Four cups and saucers 3.25" diameter.

"ME Bavaria" is the trademark, but it isn't in any marks book. It is German porcelain, and there are other sets pictured with this mold. This set came in the original box with straw in the bottom, circa 1900. It is complete with two place settings. The decoration shows large fruits, oranges, peaches, grapes, and plums with leaves. The background is brown and yellow. $400-500.

Teapot 3.5" high,
Creamer and open sugar bowl,
Two plates 5.25" diameter,
Two cups and saucers 4.12" diameter.

"ME Bavaria" is the mark on this tea service. This company produced quite a few sets using this mold. This decoration on the set shows oriental scenes. There are two women and a child dressed in Kimonos. The smaller decals are oriental flowers, vases and a butterfly. $400-500.

Teapot 3.62" high,
Creamer and open sugar bowl,
Six plates 5.25" diameter,
Six cups and saucers 4.25" diameter.

This German porcelain tea set is almost all gold overlay. Only the leaves and lilies of the valley have been left white. It is a striking set. B is impressed with the mold number but there is not enough information to identify the maker. $200-300.

Teapot 5.25" high,
Creamer 2.75" high,
Sugar 3.25" high,
One cup and saucer 3.75" diameter.

"ME Bavaria" is the trademark on this set, which would most likely date early twentieth century, but the company bearing these initials is unknown. The center decal is Santa Claus and three elves helpers loading toys into a bag on a sleigh, with one reindeer hooked up to the sleigh. It is an unusual Santa Claus set. The background colors are pink to blue-gray crooked lines to give it a rainbow effect. $800-1200.

Teapot 4" high,
Creamer and open sugar bowl,
Four cups and saucers 4.25" diameter.

Germany produced some interesting porcelain dishes, often unmarked from the manufacturer. The only mark on this set is the printed number 14, which was probably a mold code. This set would date early twentieth century. The tea set has ridges on all the pieces and is decorated with small floral decals and gold trim. $200-300.

    Teapot 4.5" high,
    Creamer and covered sugar bowl,
    Two plates 5" diameter,
    Two cups and saucers 4.12" diameter.

This German tea set came in the original box with place settings for six. It is more unusual to find German tea sets than coffee sets. This would date around the 1880s because of the large creamer and sugar bowl, keeping in mind that the sugar was not as refined as it is now. It is decorated with decals of large pink flowers and green leaves. Gold floral designs complete the decorations. $300-400.

    Teapot 4.5" high,
    Creamer 3" high,
    Covered sugar bowl 4" high,
    Six plates 6" diameter,
    Six cups and saucers 4.5" diameter.

This porcelain tea set has nursery rhymes printed on the face of the pieces. Some pieces only have the first line. The mold is similar to a set that is trademarked Czechoslovakia. $250-350.

    "Tom, Tom The Pipers Son"
    "Ride A Cock Horse"
    "Jack & Jill went Up the Hill"
    "Here We Go Round The Mulberry Bush"
    "Little Miss Muffet"
    "Cinderella and The Fairy Godmother"
    "Babes in the Wood"
    "Robinson Crusoe"

Teapot 4.5" high,
Creamer and sugar bowl,
Six plates 4" diameter,
Six cups and saucers 3.5" diameter.

This German porcelain tea set has unusual shapes using molds with embossing. It is decorated with pink luster and gold trim on the front of the pieces and has gold handles, teapot spout, finials, and rims. $150-250.

    Teapot 5" high,
    Creamer and sugar bowl,
    Four cups and saucers 4.5" diameter.

"BAVARIA" is marked on this tea set. This is a common porcelain mold decorated with decals of circus scenes. It would date about 1910 to 1914. The teapot pictures a clown riding a wild boar. The sugar bowl has a goat jumping through a hoop. The creamer has a monkey pulling a dog in a wheelbarrow, and one cup shows a clown sitting on a large ball. $250-350.

> Teapot 4.75" high,
> Creamer and sugar bowl,
> Four cups and saucers 4.25" diameter.

"BAVARIA" in gold letters is the marking on this tea set. It is decorated with decals of kittens: three kittens are playing a horn, an accordion and one reading music. Other scenes show two kittens with flowers, two kittens reading, and two kittens with a ball and drum. It is also decorated with blue and gold luster on each piece. This is a partial set. $125-175.

> Teapot 5" high,
> Creamer 2.5" high,
> Two plates 6" diameter.

This German tea set is decorated with decals of chickens. More cups are shown to feature the different breeds of chickens. $300-400.

> Teapot 5" high,
> Six cups and saucers 4.5" diameter.

This German porcelain tea set features three different breeds of chickens. The outer rim is caramel luster. The set needs a teapot. $200-300.

> Creamer 2.5" high,
> Sugar 3" high,
> Six plates 5.25" diameter,
> Six cups and saucers 4" diameter.

98

This German porcelain tea set pictures an African boy sitting on a zebra eating a banana. Other animals include a lion, an elephant, and a kangaroo. It is heavy porcelain that is a little crude, but the animals make it desirable. $100-150.
    Teapot 3.5" diameter,
    Creamer and sugar bowl,
    Two cups and saucers 3.5" diameter.

This tea set belonged to a little Dutch girl, Wilhelmina Russon, who was born in 1896 and received it as a small child. It now belongs to her granddaughter, Paula Gerdes. It is German porcelain with cobalt blue. The flowers are hand-painted. There is relief under the flowers. Gold trim completes the decoration. $300-400.
    Teapot 3.5" high,
    Creamer and covered sugar bowl,
    Six cups and saucers 3.75" diameter.

This German porcelain tea set is very attractive in cobalt blue with portraits.
There is one style of portrait on the teapot and another style on the other pieces. $250-350.
    Teapot 3.62" high,
    Creamer and covered sugar bowl,
    Four cups and saucers 3.75" diameter.

"SMITTY" is the name of this tea set that is marked "Made In Germany." It is from a comic strip created by Walter Berndt in 1922. The characters include Smitty, Herby, Mr. Bailey and the dog Scraps. This same mold was used for a "Gasoline Alley" tea set. $300-400.
    Teapot 4" high,
    Creamer and sugar bowl,
    Six plates 4.25" diameter,
    Six cups and saucers 3.75" diameter.

The only marking on this set is the decorator's number 721/866. The shapes with the dome covers, the tall creamer with a wide lip, the cobalt color, orange and gold trim, and a slight tint in the porcelain are features that seem to attribute this to German. It is beautifully decorated with cobalt trim, orange flowers and gold embellishments, which date the set about the 1880s to early 1900s. $325-400.

Teapot 4.75" high,
Creamer and sugar bowl,
Cake plate 5" diameter,
Four cups and saucers 4.25" diameter.

This German cobalt blue set is decorated with wonderful decals of cupids. Gold trim and rims make it complete. $300-400.
Teapot 3.75" high,
Creamer and sugar bowl,
Four cups and saucers 3.75" diameter.

This set is marked with a ship and below that "HOLLAND" but the pattern is on German porcelain dishes. The saucers have scalloped edges. The figures look like a transfer outline that was hand-painted and glazed over the top. The teapot shows two girls. The creamer has a boy and girl, and the cups have two boys. $250-350.
Teapot 3.62" high,
Creamer,
Four cups and saucers 4.5" diameter.

This German porcelain set came in the original red box called "Daisy Tea Set." These sets usually came with painting in silver or gold over the glaze. The painting would wear or wash off. The nice feature is that it came with a serving bowl. It was an inexpensive set, sold through mail order or dime stores around the early 1900s. $75-125.
Teapot 3.5" high,
Creamer and covered sugar bowl,
Serving bowl 4" long.
Two cups and saucers 3.25" diameter.

Germany produced numerous sets that are not trademarked. There may have been information on the boxes, but they have been destroyed long ago. This set has romantic scenes with green bands and little rose flowers. Gold trim completes the decoration. It would date early twentieth century. The plates and bowls are reticulated (pierced work). $200-300.

    Teapot 3.75" high,
    Creamer and sugar bowl,
    Two bowls 3" diameter,
    Six plates 3.25" diameter,
    Six cups and saucers 2.5" diameter.

This German set is made of good quality porcelain dating about 1900. The decorations are hand-painted and on the creamer and cups they are opposite the handles. It is trimmed with gold decorations and rims, which are worn. $100-200.

    Teapot 4" high,
    Creamer and covered sugar bowl,
    Six cups and saucers 3.5" diameter.

This unmarked sweet set looks like German porcelain. It is decorated with red roses, pink ribbons and green leaves. Gold sponged rims complete the setting. It would date in the early twentieth century. $200-300.

    Teapot 4.5" high,
    Creamer and sugar bowl,
    Cake plate 5.25" diameter,
    Six plates 4.5" diameter,
    Six cups and saucers 4" diameter.

This set is very impressive. There is no mark. The pottery is thin and made in extremely fine molds. This is a set you would like to handle. The finish of the bases is exceptionally fine. The color is gray in art deco style. It would date in the early 1900s. $200-300.

    Teapot 3.5" high,
    Creamer and sugar bowl,
    Four plates 4.25" diameter,
    Four cups and saucers 3" diameter.

German companies produced some fine sets that are not trademarked or even have the country of origin. This is a small coffee set with heavy floral embossing. There is shading from pink to yellow. The serving pieces and cups are footed. $150-200.
    Coffee pot 4.25" high,
    Creamer and sugar bowl,
    One cup and saucer 4" diameter.

This smaller scale coffee set is quite elegant porcelain with embossed molding and soft decorations. It is pure white porcelain decorated with fine decals of soft pink and blue florals. All the edges are scalloped. Gold feathering completes the decoration. $400-600.
    Coffee pot 5.25" high,
    Sugar bowl 3.6" high,
    Four plates 4" diameter,
    Four cups and saucers 3.5" diameter.

German porcelain was used to make this charming coffee set. It has a light yellow luster background with triangles in pink and gold trim. There is embossing on all the pieces. $200-300.
    Coffee pot 4.75" high,
    Creamer and sugar bowl,
    Two cups and saucers 4" diameter.

This coffee service is typical of German sets made before World War I in 1914. It is heavily embossed on porcelain pieces. The molds are exceptionally fine with ornate handles and nice decal decorations. The scenes include a windmill and a cottage; a church and cottage; and ships. $500-700.
    Coffee pot 6" high,
    Creamer and sugar bowl,
    Six cups and saucers 4.62" diameter.

Another German porcelain set in the same mold as the sinful pigs has decals of kittens. The plates have more embossing but the serving pieces are the same mold decorated with pink luster trim. The plates are 5 inches in diameter.
Price for a full set of six place settings $600-800.

This German porcelain coffee set displays decals of lions and tigers as the theme. One decal is a male and female lion, and the other decal is a tiger standing and a tiger lying down. The porcelain mold is embossed and trimmed with pink luster and gold trim. The same transfers were used on some R.S. Prussia wares, but other porcelain manufacturers could have bought the same decals for their decorations. $1600-2000.
Coffee pot 6" high,
Creamer 3.5" high,
Sugar bowl 4" high,
Six cups and saucers 4.5" diameter.

This is a lovely German porcelain mold with heavy embossing and pink luster trim. The decorations are known as the sinful pigs. The decals have two pigs smoking. Another scene includes two pigs rolling dice. The third scene shows three pigs sitting at a table drinking. The decal makers had a good sense of humor. $1200-1400.
Coffee pot 6" high,
Creamer 3.35" high,
Covered sugar bowl 4" high,
Six plates 5.25" diameter,
Six cups and saucers 4.25" diameter.

This German porcelain coffee service is decorated with elephants. There are sayings on the face of the pieces that include "Jumbo At Football," "Jumbo Rinking" (roller-skating), "Jumbo Playing Tennis," "Good Luck Old Boy" (kayaking). The molds are exceptionally nice with fancy handles and embossing. The decals make this an interesting, colorful set. $500-700.
Coffee pot 6" high,
Creamer 3" high,
Sugar bowl 4" high,
Six plates 6" diameter,
Six cups and saucers 4.5" diameter.

This plate is trademarked "Orla, GERMANY" dating about 1900. The decal pictures two lions. It has a green luster border. You can just imagine a full set with wild animals. This decal was used by R.S. Prussia. Plate $50-75.

    Plate 5.5" diameter.

This exceptional German porcelain coffee service would be a joy to own. It has a soft pink background with bright pink flowers and blue sprays of flowers. The decals are well placed and with heavy gold trim. This set has lovely molds with embossing and scalloped edges, circa 1910. $400-600.

    Coffee pot 6" high,
    Creamer and covered sugar bowl,
    Three cups and saucers 4.5" diameter.

This German porcelain coffee set is decorated with circus scenes. They are decals on a nice mold shape. There are many decals depicting the circus, which include animals and acts. $300-400.

    Coffee pot 6" high,
    Creamer and sugar bowl,
    Six cups and saucers 4.25" diameter.

Germany produced some fine porcelain sets with exceptional moldings, circa 1910. This set is decorated with decals of little girls in three different poses. Two little girls are dressed in purple and yellow dresses or purple and white dresses. All the edges of the pieces are scalloped. $400-600.

    Coffee pot 5.75" high,
    Creamer 2.5" high,
    Sugar bowl 3.5" high,
    Six plates 6" diameter,
    Six cups and saucers 4.6" diameter.

This three-piece coffee set is typical of the type of German porcelain sets produced around the turn of the twentieth century. It is decorated with multicolor flowers and gold rims. $100-150.
 Coffee pot 6" high,
 Creamer 3.5" high,
 Sugar bowl.

This is a lovely German porcelain mold that is decorated with pink roses and green leaves. The edges are trimmed with gold. It has heavy embossing with beautiful handles. This mold was used with many different decorations. $300-500.
 Coffee pot 6" high,
 Tall creamer 3.75" high,
 Large sugar bowl 4" high,
 Six plates 5" diameter,
 Six cups and saucers 4.25" diameter.

This German coffee service has vertical ridges in the mold. It is decorated with very nice decals of children. The saucers have small circus scenes. It has gold rims and touches of gold. $400-500.
 Coffee pot 5.75" high,
 Creamer and sugar bowl,
 Six cups and saucers 4.5" diameter.

"GERMANY" is the only marking on this beautiful porcelain coffee service. It has six sides and embossed trim with porcelain dots. It is decorated with yellow roses, green leaves and a little bright pink luster trim. $400-500.
 Coffee pot 6.5" high,
 Creamer and sugar bowl,
 Six plates 5" diameter,
 Six cups and saucers 4.5" diameter.

"GERMANY" is stamped on the base of these pieces. It is very nice porcelain heavily embossed with a beading effect on the base, around the base of the spout and the top rim. The top portion of the pieces has luster added. The flowers are purple shades of crocus with green leaves and brown at the base of the stems. $500-700.

> Coffee pot 6.25" high,
> Creamer 3.5" high,
> Covered sugar bowl,
> Six cups and saucers 4.5" diameter.

GERMANY

The trademarks include "GERMANY, SILESIA, P NS," "Franz Prause, Nieder-Salzbrunn," which are the manufacturer and the city. The Franz Prause Company used this mark from 1910 to 1935. It is nice porcelain decorated with scenes of children. $400-500.

> Coffee pot 6.25" high,
> Creamer and sugar bowl,
> Four plates 4" diameter,
> Four cups and saucers 4.12" diameter.

"GERMANY" is marked in a circle on this set's base. This is a beautiful mold with embossing and exquisite handles. There are decals of two children and a dog watching a parrot. Other scenes include three children in a garden setting, and a girl handing a pretzel to two other children. The set includes a sugar bowl and an extra bowl, for sugar lumps, or jams. $400-500.

> Coffee pot 6" high,
> Creamer and sugar bowl,
> Extra open bowl,
> Four cups and saucers 4.25" diameter.

This is an interesting German cup that most likely came out of a coffee service. The decal is a black boy with small ducks. $35-65.

> Cup 2.25" high.

Buster Brown is the theme on this small coffee service. Each piece has a different hand-painted design. It is German porcelain made for the American market. One cup displays the American flag. It may have been sold as white ware and decorated in the United States. $500-700.
  Coffee server 4.25" high,
  Creamer and sugar bowl,
  Five cups and saucers 3.75" high.

"MADE IN GERMANY" in a circle mark is on this coffee set. It is decorated with silhouettes. The figures are formal styles of a man and woman in the late 1800s. The man is handing flowers to the woman. $300-400.
  Coffee pot 5.75" high,
  Creamer and sugar bowl,
  Five plates 4.5" diameter,
  Five cups.

This German porcelain set has embossed molds. The cup has moldings around the center decal. The saucer has molding outlined in gold trim. The decals show a little girl in a fancy purple dress and wide brim hat. The shapes are well proportioned in the serving pieces and saucers, but the cups are a large mug shape. $250-350.
  Coffee pot 5.5" high,
  Creamer 3.5" high,
  Covered sugar bowl 3" high,
  One cup and one saucer 4.25" diameter.

This German porcelain coffee service is decorated with silhouettes. The decorators have added color: the boy's shirt is blue and the girl has a green apron. There is also a little dog in the setting. Green trim completes the setting. $250-350.
  Coffee server 5.5" high,
  Creamer and sugar bowl,
  Four cups and saucers 4.5" diameter.

The maker of this coffee service is Waldsassen Bareuther & Co. A.G. from Waldsassen, Germany, dating about 1920. It is decorated with decals of black silhouette children, dogs, rabbits, goats, geese, pigeons and cats. Some color has been added to the decals. Gold trim and rims complete the decoration. $250-350.
> Coffee pot 5.5" high,
> Creamer and covered sugar bowl,
> Open sugar bowl,
> Four cups and saucers 4.5" diameter.

This German porcelain coffee service is decorated with a center medallion. It has a light blue background with a white animal in the center. The coffee pot has a rabbit on the front and a gorilla on the back. The creamer has a cat on the front and a horse on the back. $250-350.
> Coffee pot 5.75" high,
> Creamer 4" high,
> Four cups and saucers 4.25" diameter.

This German porcelain set is not marked. It is decorated with dark pink edges and gold trim. The handles and coffee pot spout are all gold. $150-250.
> Coffee pot 6" high,
> Creamer and sugar bowl,
> Serving plate 4.75" diameter,
> Four plates 3.75" diameter,
> Four cups and saucers 3.75" diameter.

"GERMANY" is the marking on this coffee set. The mold is very nice with embossing on all the pieces. It is decorated with decals of circus scenes. They are: A clown with a dog and another dog jumping through a hoop; a monkey riding a horse while the ringleader and trainer are standing; an acrobat with two dogs; an elephant standing on a pedestal; a horse sitting and a dog sitting up. Around the edges are small decorative decals of clowns, clown heads, a horse head, or a ball. $400-600.
> Coffee pot 6" high,
> Creamer 3.5" high,
> Covered sugar bowl,
> Six plates 5.25" diameter,
> Six cups and saucers 4" diameter.

These plates of this set came from a coffee service with a common mold but different decals. The scenes include two Dutch girls in each decal. They are very colorful in their native dress. The set would date early 1900s. $400-500.

     Coffee pot 6" high,
     Creamer and sugar bowl,
     Six plates 5" diameter,
     Six cups and saucers.

This German porcelain set features the Teaching Bears or Busy Bears. It shows the schoolmaster with four bears; bears playing leapfrog; and bears drawing a picture of the teacher on the wall. This is the same decal as other sets on a different mold. It is also decorated with deep pink luster dating it early 1900s. $400-500.

     Coffee pot 5.5" high,
     Creamer and sugar bowl,
     Four cups and saucers 3.5" diameter.

This is another nice porcelain coffee service dating about 1920. The decals include a dog pulling off a girl's sock; a girl playing with a toy elephant and doll; and a girl with her teddy bear. It is finished with gold rims. $200-300.
     Coffee pot 6.25" high,
     Creamer and covered sugar bowl,
     Six cups and saucers 5.62" diameter.

This German porcelain coffee set has decals of bears. The mold is very nice with ornate handles. There are three different scenes decorating this set. One scene shows two bears playing leapfrog with a third bear looking around the fence. In another scene a bear is drawing "teacher" on the fence while the teacher is looking from behind the fence. In the third scene the teacher is sitting with a book teaching four bears to read. This set is missing its creamer and sugar bowl. $200-300.

     Coffee pot 5.25" high,
     Two plates 5" diameter,
     Two cups and saucers 4.5" diameter.

Mitterteich AG in Metterteich, Bavaria, Germany, is the maker of this porcelain coffee service dating about 1935. It is good quality porcelain decorated with decals of children playing. The molds are octagonal with unique handles. Gold trim completes the decoration. $200-300.
    Coffee pot 7.25" high,
    Creamer and covered sugar bowl,
    Six cups and saucers 4.25" diameter.

"Porzellanfabrik Arzberg, Arzberg Bayern" is on the trademark. Porzellanfabrik means porcelain factory and Bayern means Bavaria, which is a province in Germany. This mark was used from 1930 until 1947. This set dates from around 1935. Other factories, including the Dutch factory Société Céramique, used the same decals. The gnome is pictured with different animals, riding a snail and dragonfly, and talking to a goose and a frog. The set is trimmed with an orange band. $200-300.
    Coffee pot 5.75" high,
    Creamer and covered sugar bowl,
    Four cups and saucers 4.5" diameter.

"GERMANY" is the only marking on this tea set. It is a common mold that was used with numerous different decals. The decals are of dressed animals with sayings on the pieces. $350-550.
"Said Leo, when in town, I'll stop at Foxes fine new barber's shop," "This is the way policeman tray stops traffic on a busy day," and "The smallest scholar learns with ease to spell the name of every cheese."
    Teapot 5.5" high,
    Creamer and covered sugar bowl,
    Four plates 4.25" diameter,
    Four cups and saucers 4.25" diameter.

"Leuchtenburg" and a little castle is on the trademark of this set. This porcelain coffee set was made by C. A. Lehman & Sohn, Kahla, Leuchtenburg, Germany, about 1930. The mark was used from 1910 until 1935. They used nice molds with some embossing. The decals picture a boy and girl with tennis items with the boy giving the girl a bouquet of flowers; two children with a little sailing boat; and two children one on skis and the other on a sleigh. The set is finished with gold trim. $200-300.
    Coffee pot 6.37" high,
    Creamer and covered sugar bowl,
    Four cups and saucers 4.25" diameter.

This German porcelain coffee service is decorated in iridescent luster with red sponge trim. The handles and coffeepot spout are white with gold trim. Only the front of the pieces is decorated. It would date early 1900s. $200-300.
  Coffee pot 6" high,
  Creamer and sugar bowl,
  Six plates 5.25" diameter,
  Six cups and saucers 4.25" diameter. a

This is a common German mold that was used with numerous different decorations dating early 1900s. The sayings on the front of the pieces include: "Charlie and Charlotte went one day, out for a day and lost their way," and "This is the way policeman tray, stops traffic on a busy day." This set was made for export because the captions are written in English. $300-400.
  Teapot 5.25" high,
  Creamer and sugar bowl,
  Four cups and saucers 4" diameter.

"Three Crown China, GERMANY" in a circle is the given trademark. No information was found on this mark but it should be from around 1910. It is an interesting mold with embossing. The decorations are decals of large bold fruits. The luster trim is light orange and green. The serving plate pictures two pears with cherries and flowers. $400-600.
  Coffee pot 5.6" high,
  Creamer and sugar bowl both 3.25" high,
  Four plates 5.25" diameter,
  Four cups and saucers 4.12" diameter.

This coffee service is using a common mold but the decorations are decals of children from about the 1920s. It has interesting decals on each piece. "MADE IN GERMANY" is printed on the bottom. $250-350.
  Coffee server 5.25" high,
  Creamer and sugar bowl,
  Six plates 5" diameter,
  Six cups and saucers 4.25" diameter.

This German porcelain set is decorated in a simple design referred to as "Straw Flower." Variations of this set came on different molds in many sizes from child's play to medium or small doll dishes. $75-150.
    Teapot 3.75" high,
    Sugar bowl,
    Four plates 3.25" diameter,
    Four cups and saucers 3" diameter.

This German tea set is in the original box with excelsior packing (fine curled wood shavings). It is painted over the glaze with metallic gold and red. Only the front of the pieces are decorated. The backs are white. The molds have relief designs but the painting does not follow the molds. This color painting is in the style of Goofus Glass dating about 1900. Goofus Glass was painted with cheap gold color paint. $175-250.
    Teapot 3.5" high,
    Creamer and sugar bowl,
    Six plates 3.5" diameter,
    Six cups and saucers 3.5" diameter.

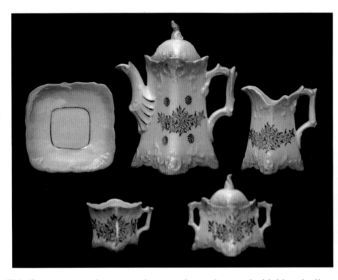

This German tea set has unusual square shapes decorated with blue shading on the top and bottom. The center has a gold floral pattern. $100-200.
    Teapot 5.37" high,
    Creamer and sugar bowl,
    Six cups and saucers 3.25" diameter.

"Germani" spelled with an "I" is impressed on the back of the teapot. The serving pieces are especially nice examples of clowns. The covers on the teapot and sugar bowl are clown heads with a small black top hat. The handles and teapot spout are arms of the clown. The cups have an embossed clown hand-painted. This set also came in a dark green color. $400-600.
    Teapot 3.5" high,
    Creamer and covered sugar bowl,
    Two cups and saucers 2.5" high.

This set is marked with a registry number "Rd No 360874." The set looks like German porcelain that was intended for the English market. This number would date the set in 1900. This is one of the most unusual molds of all the children's play dishes. It is in the shape of a peach. The teapot is footed, in the shape of a peach, with a green leaf-shaped spout and a twig-shape handle. The cover is a flower with petals. The creamer, sugar, and cups match with leaves and twigs. The saucers are square with green molded leaves and flower on each corner. It is fine porcelain in beautiful condition. $400-500.

   Teapot 4" high,
   Creamer 3" high,
   Open sugar bowl,
   Two cups and saucers 4" square.

"Germany" is impressed on the bottom of the tea service pieces. The box is marked "Toy Tea Set." The figural birds are crude for German wares. Originally the set sold for $1.00 and was sent parcel post for fifteen cents, dated August 22, 1927. $75-125.

   Teapot 4.25" high,
   Creamer and sugar bowl,
   Six cups and saucers 3.25" diameter.

This is another figural set is in the shape of chickens. It is German porcelain hand-painted in bright colors of green, yellow, blue, red, and black. The painting is over the glaze and does show wear. $150-250.

   Teapot 4" high,
   Creamer and sugar bowl,
   Four cups and saucers 3.25" diameter.

This German tea set is in the shape of strawberries with leaves. The handles and finial are in the shape of stems. The saucers are leaves. It is extremely fine thin porcelain. The molds and coloring are exceptional. $350-500.

   Teapot 4" high,
   Creamer and open sugar bowl,
   Two cups and saucers 4" diameter.

"Germany" is printed on the base of these pieces. It is a beverage set that almost matches the bottom set. $300-400.

 Pitcher 6" high,
 Four cups 1.5" high.

Germany produced some interesting figural tea sets. This set is in the shape and colors of a peach. It is shaded from yellow to orange with green leaves and brown stems for the finial, handles and teapot spout. $200-300.

 Teapot 3.5" high,
 Creamer and sugar bowl,
 Six cups and saucers 4.25" diameter.

This German set must be for apple cider. The tray has embossing in the shape of leaves. The cider pot and cups are in the shape of apples. The stopper on the spout is an apple. It would date about 1900. $400-500.

 Tray 7.5" diameter,
 Cider pot 4.25" high,
 Four cups 1.37" high.

This figural set is in the shape of peaches or apricots. It is a better quality because it is decorated all the way around the pieces. It is a bold set with the fruit and dark green leaves including gold rub on the leaves. $200-300.

 Coffee pot 6" high,
 Creamer and sugar bowl,
 Four cups and saucers 4" diameter.

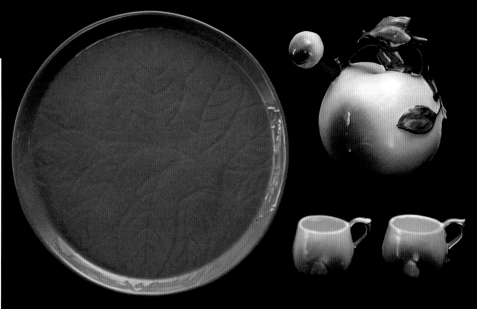

Some German sets were made as a novelty item rather than a quality set. This one is in the shape of peaches with leaves and stems. It would have been a cheaper set with painting done over the glaze. The fronts have been decorated to show off in the display box and the backs of the pieces are plain white. $150-250.

    Coffee pot 5.75" high,
    Creamer and covered sugar bowl,
    Two cups and saucers 4" diameter.

This German porcelain set is in the shape of a melon. It is orange with green stems and leaves. The quality is average. The open sugar bowl has an attached leaves base. $150-250.

    Teapot 3.75" high,
    Creamer and open sugar bowl,
    One cup.

This grape figural set is in the shape of a bunch of purple grapes. The handles are the brown twigs and the leaves are green with gold trim. It was only painted on the front to look nice in a display box. The backs are white. It is not as good a quality as some of the other fruit molds. $150-250.

    Coffee pot 5" high,
    Creamer and sugar bowl,
    Four cups and saucers 4" by 4.5".

This set is trademarked "B Prussia, Gesetzlich Geschutzl." The company is Beyer and Bock. They used this mark between 1922 and 1930. The set was especially attractive because of the unusual shapes, in the designs of the 1920s. It has unique covers and pointed handles. It is nicely decorated with decals of pink flowers and greens. $400-500.

    Teapot 4.82" high,
    Creamer and covered sugar bowl,
    One cup and saucer 4.25" diameter.

The maker of this coffee service is Georg Schmider Vereinigte Zeller Keramische Fabriken (George Schmider United Zeller Ceramic Factories) that is located in Zell am Hamersbach, Germany. The trademark also says "handgemalt" meaning hand-painted. The name of the set is "Henne Und Hahn" (Hen and Cock). The set was made in 1989. In Germany and the Netherlands this service is also available for adults and is very popular. $100-200.

 Coffee pot 6" high,
 Creamer and open sugar bowl,
 Four cups and saucers 4.75" diameter.

"MADE IN GERMANY" is the mark on this coffee set. The only decoration is bright orange luster with black handles, finials, and coffeepot spout. The reason for picturing this set is that it could be mistaken for Japanese. $200-300.

 Coffee pot 5.75" high,
 Creamer and covered sugar,
 Six cups and saucers 4.25" diameter.

"P. T., Bavaria, Tirschenreuth" is given on the trademark. This is a very nice porcelain set decorated in caramel luster with black handles and trim. $200-300.

 Coffee server 5.75" high,
 Creamer and sugar bowl,
 Four plates 6" diameter,
 Four cups and saucers 4" diameter.

"G S Zell, BADEN" is on the trademark. This mark was used by Georg Schmider from 1906 to 1922. It was most likely made for the Dutch market. The creamer is unusual with the handle on the side. The colors are bright on this attractive set of Dutch scenes. $400-500.

 Pitcher 3.62" high,
 Creamer and open sugar bowl,
 Four plates 6" diameter,
 Four cups and saucers 4.75" diameter.

Retsch & Co., Wunsiedel, Bavaria, Germany is the maker of this coffee set dating about 1955. This porcelain set is decorated with decals of children; a boy is offering a girl a bouquet of flowers; and a boy playing a flute while the girl is singing. The trim and the finials are gold. $150-250.
   Coffee pot 6.37" high,
   Creamer and covered sugar bowl,
   Four cups and saucers 4.74" square.

This porcelain coffee service was made by Schirnding in Schirnding, Bavaria, Germany. They used this trademark from 1948 until 1974. The date of this set would be about 1965. "Qualitats Porzellan" on the trademark means quality porcelain. It is decorated with decals of children; a girl caressing a frog; a girl and a boy playing tennis; and a girl fishing. $100-200.
   Coffee pot 7.25" high,
   Creamer and covered sugar bowl,
   Four cups and saucers 4.75" diameter.

This is a late twentieth century German porcelain set. It has unusual molds in bold green and white stripe. Gold rims and finials complete the decoration. $50-100.
   Teapot 3" high,
   Creamer and sugar bowl,
   Two cups and saucers 2.5" by 3".

This porcelain coffee set is made by Creidlitz, Bavaria, Eastern-Germany about 1960. The decals are gnomes wearing different clothes, but all have a red cap and a lantern. The rims are painted gold. $100-200.
   Coffee pot 6.5" high,
   Creamer and covered sugar bowl,
   Six cups and saucers 4.5" diameter.

"Made In Western-Germany" is printed on the base, which would date the set between 1949 and 1989. The set is cobalt blue decorated with cheap gold color paint over the glaze. $100-200.

Teapot 4.25" diameter,
Creamer and sugar bowl,
Four cups and saucers 3.25" diameter.

The information on the box of this set is "Roehler Collection, Made In Germany, Fine Porcelain." This is a typical mold made from about the 1980s. This set is included because of the Christmas decorations. There is St. Nicholas with a sack of toys, a bag of sticks, a little girl with a doll, and a Christmas Tree. $200-300.

Teapot 6.5" high,
Creamer and sugar bowl,
Four cups and saucers 4" diameter.

"Metropolitan Museum of Art, Made by Reutter Porzellan, W. Germany" is the information given on this tea service. It is from the 1990s. $100-150. The verse on the back of the teapot is "Polly put the kettle on." The verses on the plates are:

"Here am I,
Little Jumping Joan
When nobody's with me,
I'm always alone."

"Little Tom Tucker
Sang for his supper
What did he sing for,
White bread & butter
How can I cut it without a knife?
How can I marry without a wife?"

"Little Bo-Peep
Has lost her sheep
And doesn't know where to find them.
Leave them alone
And they'll come home
And bring their tails behind them."

"Little Miss Muffet
Sat on a tuffet
Eating some curds and whey.
Then came a great spider
And sat down beside her
And frightened Miss Muffet away."

Teapot 5" high,
Creamer and sugar bowl,
Four plates 7" diameter,
Four cups and saucers 4.5" diameter.

This "Alice in Wonderland" porcelain tea set was made for the New York Public Library and the Metropolitan Museum Of Art in 1993. The information below was included with the set. It was made by Reutter Porcelain Co. in Germany. It includes two place settings with the teapot, but no creamer or sugar bowl. Sayings on the pieces include "Oh dear! Oh dear! I shall be too late!" and "It's a friend of mine–a Cheshire-cat, allow me to introduce it, said Alice." $40-80.

Teapot 4.87" high,
Two plates 6.75" diameter,
Two cups and saucers 4.5" diameter.

This porcelain teaset is decorated with applied decal design. The Color has been added.
© NYPL MMA 1993
Reutter Porzellan Made in Germany

The next six sets were made in Germany for the Netherlands market. The Dutch Van Nelle Company sold coffee, tea, and related items. Every year the company issued a catalog that showed the items you could purchase, (such as coffee makers, adult tea services, coffee and tea spoons, and children's dishes) with tokens (coupons) from Van Nelle products.

This tea set is made of porcelain with "Van Nelle" printed on each piece. This is the fourth child's set offered by this company. You could buy it for 2000 tokens from 1971 to 1973. The decorations are little bouquets of flowers and gold trim. $75-150.

Teapot 3.87" high,
Creamer and covered sugar bowl,
Four cups and saucers 3.75" diameter.

Paddington Bear ™
Reutter Porzellan
Germany
®Paddington and company Ltd 1998
Licensed by Copyrights Europe

"Paddington Bear™" is printed on this tea set by Reutter Porzellan, Germany. Other information is "®Paddington and Company Ltd. 1998, Licensed by Copyrights Europe." Paddington was a character from the book *A Bear Called Paddington* by Michael Bond. In the story, Paddington was a stowaway bear from Peru. Mr. & Mrs. Brown found him at Paddington Station in London and gave him that name. They took him home for their children Jonathan and Judy. This porcelain tea set for two was packed in the picnic basket with flatware and napkins. $50-100.

Teapot 3.5" high,
Creamer and sugar bowl,
Two plates 3.75" diameter
Two cups and saucers 2.75" diameter.

Van Nelle Company offered this set from 1982 to 1985. The little gnome on the coffee set is called "Piggelmee." His character was exclusively created for the Van Nelle company and is well known in the Netherlands. The Piggelmee character was introduced in 1920 and first appeared in books. This set could be purchased with 5000 tokens. It is decorated with decals and gold trim. $75-150.

    Coffee pot 4.87" high,
    Creamer and open sugar bowl,
    Four cups and saucers 3.37" diameter.

The Dutch company of Douwe Egberts is another company selling tea, coffee, and other products. Every year they issued a catalog of items for sale or items that you could order with coupons. Kahla in Eastern Germany made the first Douwe Egberts child's set offered from 1975 to 1977. They called it "India Blauw" (blue). On the teapot handle is a little mark, "DE," in blue, which means that this service was exclusively made for Douwe Egberts. $75-150.

    Teapot 3.25" high,
    Creamer and open sugar bowl,
    Four cups and saucers 3.5" diameter.

Rosler, Bavaria, Western Germany, is the maker of this thick porcelain coffee set dating 1990 to 1994. "Piggelmee en de Keulse Pot" (Piggelmee and the Cologne jar) is the name of this set and is printed on the serving pieces and cups. The pictures are showing Piggelmee standing beside the Cologne jar. The edges are trimmed with gold. This is the eighth and last set Van Nelle gave in exchange for their tokens. $75-150.

    Coffee pot 5" high,
    Creamer and covered sugar bowl,
    Four cups and saucers 3.87" diameter.

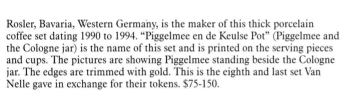

Kahla in Eastern Germany made this set for Douwe Egberts from 1988 to 1990. It was the fourth children's set for this company. The quality is not as good as in the previous sets. The decorations are panda bears with gold trim. $75-150.

    Coffee server 5.25" high,
    Creamer and covered sugar bowl,
    Four cups and saucers 3.5" diameter.

This German tête-à-tête set is made of beautiful porcelain, using an exceptional mold. There is heavy embossing on all the pieces. The teapot handle is delicate and it's a miracle that it was never broken. It is decorated with light blue shading and little soft flowers. It all fits on the lovely tray. $300-400.

Tray approximately 8" by 12",
Teapot 5.5" high to top of handle,
Creamer and sugar bowl,
Two cups and saucers 4" diameter.

Roehler from Germany is the maker of this coffee set for Douwe Egberts. It is the sixth set they offered for their tokens, from 1998 until now. "Nijntje" is the name of the little rabbit pictured on this set. In the United States she is called "Miffy." She was created by a Dutch artist, Dick Bruna, about fifty years ago. The decals are of Nijntje, a cow, a hen, a cock, and a sheep. The plates and saucers are decorated with little flowers around the rim. $75-150.

Coffee pot 4.37" high,
Creamer and open sugar bowl,
Four plates 4" diameter,
Four cups and saucers 3.5" diameter

This German porcelain tea set on a tray is of fair quality. It is decorated with pink, touches of cobalt, and gold. Only the front of the pieces are decorated. $125-200.

Tray 7.37" by 9.5",
Teapot 4.75" high,
Creamer and sugar bowl,
Two cups and saucers 4" diameter.

"J P F, Germany" is on the trademark, which stands for the Limenauer Porcelain Co. located in Thuringen. This mark was used from 1903 to 1933. This set is bold pink with hand-painted gold over the embossing. It is decorated with soft floral decals. It is shaded from dark pink to green at the base of the pieces. It is a little larger than most sets and may be a demitasse set. $200-300.

Tray 8.5" by 11.25",
Teapot 4.25" high,
Sugar bowl,
Two cups and saucers 4.62" diameter.

Tête-à-tête sets are quite interesting and are a cabaret service for two persons. This one is German porcelain with cobalt blue band and gold trim. The center picture is "ANVERS, GRANDE PLACE." Anvers is the French name for Antwerp, Belgium. The center town square is pictured. The tray is an unusual shape with the picture in the center. Each of the other pieces has a smaller picture and cobalt blue trim. $150-250.

    Tray about 8" by 10",
    Teapot 4.5" high,
    Creamer and covered sugar bowl,
    Two cups and saucers 4.25" diameter.

Elfinware was designed after Dresden-like applied porcelain decorations. These pieces were sold in dime stores and gift shops. The mark was registered by Breslauer-Underberg Inc. of New York City in 1947. Pieces marked "Elfinware, Made In Germany" had been sold by this importer since 1945. This set is decorated with a pink center flower and green edge. The tray has blue flowers around the outside rim. $250-350.

    Tray 3.5" by 5.25",
    Teapot 2.25" high,
    Creamer and sugar bowl,
    Two cups and saucers 1.75" diameter.

This is a new set marked "Blue Bird, Matthew 6-26, Fuvnari's LTD., First Edition." The country of origin is not given, but it does look like it may have been made in Germany. It is decorated with blue birds and swags of flowers. The pot is shaped like a coffeepot and the cups are shaped more like mugs. The verse from the Bible is "Look at the birds of the air; they neither sow nor reap nor gather into barns, and yet your heavenly Father feeds them. Are you not of more value than they?" $75-125.

    Tray 6" by 14.75" long,
    Coffee pot 5.25" high,
    Creamer and sugar bowl,
    Two cups and saucers.

Cocoa sets are much harder to find than tea or coffee sets. This cocoa set is very attractive with pink luster and gold flowers. The mold is raised on the bases and for the flowers. The saucer has raised molding around the rim for the cup, probably dating in the late 1800s. The cocoa pot is tall with a long handle. The tall creamer and sugar bowl are a nice mold match to the cocoa pot. $400-600.

    Cocoa pot 6.5" high,
    Creamer 3.5" high,
    Covered sugar bowl 4" high,
    Six cups and saucers 3.18" diameter.

A beverage set is a unique find. This one is German porcelain from about the late 1800s. It is decorated in blue with little cherubs. The tray holds the pitcher and five little mugs. The pitcher is shaped in a triangle, the top molding looks like a pulled ribbon around the neck with a ribbon handle. The mugs picture different poses of three cherubs on each piece. $350-450.

    Tray 5.25" by 7",
    Pitcher 3" high,
    Five mugs 1.75" high.

This German porcelain beverage set was probably intended as a liquor set. It is a good size to use with children's play dishes. The carafe is heavily embossed with a floral and leaf decoration. The matching cups are perfect play size. It would date early 1900s. $100-150.

    Carafe 6" high,
    Carafe 7" high to the top of the stopper,
    Six small mugs 1.75" high.

Villeroy and Boch merged factories in 1841 and began using the V&B trademark. Their steins were imported to the United States from about 1860 to 1900. These three steins were styled after the pottery steins that were made in Mettlach, but these are not trademarked. Two of these steins have a metal hinged lid with thumblift. From the quality and coloring they would probably date about 1870s. Steins were used for beer or ale. The stein on the left shows a Roman soldier on a dark blue background. The word "ANTIOCHUS" is impressed on the front and "MAKKABEUS" is on the back. Judas Maccabeus defeated Antiochus Epiphanes during the second century BC. This is remembered during the festival of Hannukah. The stein is 4" high. The center stein shows a Roman figure on the front and back. It is beige with red and green trim. It has a pewter top. It has "HEKTOR, ACHILLES" in raised letters. It is 4.5" high. The final stein pictures a man figure. It is tan with a green background. The bottom has the word "MUSTERSCHUTE." It is 3.25" high. Each stein $100.

Fish sets are a rare find in children's play size. This set is heavy porcelain, circa 1880s. The fish and seaweed are molded in relief, then hand-painted over the molding. The edges have light green luster trim. The teapot was found separately and would be part of a matching tea set. The finial is in the shape of a fish tail.
It is not quality porcelain but interesting. A full fish set with six individual plates would be $200-300.
> Teapot 3.75" high,
> Two fish platters 3" by 5",
> Two plates 3.5" diameter.

This German dinner set was purchased in 1970 from an antique dealer in Yonkers, NY. This note was included with the set: "The set of dishes came from a very wealthy German-American family. They had antiques and wealth for three generations in America. I believe this set to have been made between 1860-1890. It never had a dessert service with it as they had a separate one. This is known as a meat service. It was actually used by a little girl to entertain her friends. The dessert service was not the same pattern. I hope you derive much pleasure from the set you purchased." This is a lovely designed porcelain dinner service. It has shades of green with floral decorations and extra gold trim. $700-800.

Large tureen 4" high,
Two smaller covered tureens 3.5" high,
Gravy boat with attached base,
Salad bowl 1.6" high by 3.75" top diameter,
Two meat dishes 3.75" by 6",
Two little condiment dishes,
Two large serving plates 6.3" diameter,
One small plate 4.6" diameter,
Six dinner plates 5.1" diameter,
Six soup plates 5.1" diameter.

This porcelain dinner set is made by Reinhold Schlegelmilch (R.S. Prussia) in Suh, Prussia, Germany, circa 1890. It is nicely decorated with a pink band and floral designs with gold rims. $300-400.

> Covered soup tureen and stand 4.37" high,
> Covered vegetable dish,
> Open bowl, meat platter,
> Pedestal dish,
> Gravy boat with attached underplate,
> Open salt & pepper dish with handle,
> Six plates 3.5" diameter.

"Entered at Stationers Hall" is printed on this tea and dinner service. The set is German porcelain for the English market, with the sayings in English. The decals are Chinese children with long pigtails. The tea set and the dinner set were sold separately. Both sets $500-700. Here are the sayings:
"Here we go all in a row, Holding on to Pigtails Ho! Ho! Ho!"
"While studying his lesson book, He fishes with his pig-tail hook." "Sometimes a teasing Chinese Boy, His fellow playmates will annoy." "You know of course, a pig-tail does to draw a horse." "When he goes to school you see, It does instead of B.A.G." "This little chinaman Chi Lung went marketing when he was young, with cash upon his pig-tail hung."

> Teapot 3.5" high,
> Creamer 2.75" high,
> One cup and saucer 3.75" diameter,
> Plate 4" diameter,
> Tureen 4.75" high,
> Covered dish 3" high,
> Open dish 2" by 3",
> Platter 3.25" by 4.5".

Entered at Stationers Hall.

These two German porcelain pieces came out of a large-sized dinner service. The decals picture a dressed kitten with a pug dog and two rats dressed in clothing. This mold was also decorated with circus scenes and a sandman theme. Full dinner service $700-900.

> Plate 5.5" diameter
> Square bowl 4.5" diameter.

"Villeroy and Boch, Dresden" is trademarked on this set. This particular mark was used between 1878 and 1945. The set is nice earthenware with blue band trim. The tureen has unique handles. All the pieces have ridges rather than a smooth finish. $400-500.
 Tureen 4.75" high,
 Large underplate 5.1" diameter,
 Sauce pitcher,
 Serving bowl 4.25" diameter,
 Meat dish 4" by 5.75",
 Five dinner plates 4" diameter,
 Five soup plates 4" diameter.

Germany is the maker of this small-sized porcelain dinner set from around 1900. It is decorated with hand-painted flowers and blue trim. The tureen finial is a bud with leaves decorated with blue trim. It would be a nice size to set a table for a doll. $100-$200.
 Tureen 4" high,
 Meat dish 3.25" by 5.25",
 Small round bowl 3.5" diameter,
 Square serving dish 3.25" square plus the handles,
 Tiny little oval dish 1.25" by 1.75",
 Six dinner plates 3" diameter.

"VILLEROY & BOCH, DRESDEN, MADE IN GERMANY" is on the trademark of this set. This company used this mark from 1878 to 1945. This set would date about the 1930s. It is earthenware decorated with orange bands. Four glass tumblers with matching rims came with the set. $400-500.
 Large covered casserole 3.5" high,
 Smaller covered casserole 2.75" high,
 Sauce pitcher,
 Platter 4.25" by 6.75",
 Four dinner plates 4.62" diameter,
 Four soup plates 4.5" diameter,
 Four glass tumblers 2.25" high.

"Liane, Waechtersbach, Made in West Germany" is the information on this set's trademark, dating it about 1950. This factory is in Schlierbach. The dinner set is decorated with a red transfer sheet pattern of branches with leaves. It is unusual and very striking with a body of lightweight earthenware. $300-400.

Soup tureen with cover 3.75" high,
Covered vegetable dish,
Gravy boat with attached underplate,
Round meat platter, salad bowl,
Small round open serving dish,
Six dinner plates and
six soup plates 3.37" diameter,
Six dessert plates 2.75" diameter.

This German dinner set is especially interesting because it came in the original box, circa 1920s. It is nice that the set is complete. There are a number of these sets, with different decorations. This set is decorated with flowers and fruits. $150-200.

Covered serving dish 3.25" high,
Platter 3" by 4.5",
Square dish 2.5" across,
Round dish 2.5" diameter,
Sauce pitcher,
Six plates 3" diameter.

This small dinner set came in the original cardboard box, which is marked "Made in Germany." The heavy porcelain pieces have embossing decorated with gold. Little flowers are the center decoration. It was made as a cheap set with uneven shapes and flaws, around the turn of the twentieth century. $75-150.

Soup tureen 2.75" high,
Ladle, open dish,
Butter boat, pickle dish,
Meat dish 2.75" by 4.25",
Six dinner plates 2.25" diameter,
Six soup bowls 1.62" diameter.

This moss rose decorated tray may be German. It has heavy reinforced porcelain bars on the bottom to make it strong. It goes well with the American "Moss Rose" coffee set pictured in this book. $50-100.

    Tray 7" by 9.5".

 K P M is the trademark for Royal Porcelain Manufactory. (German: Konigliche Porzellan Manufaktur). Royal Works in Berlin was established in 1763 and is still in production. This is a 1990s doll-sized set marked with the scepter over KPM. It is fine porcelain with blue floral center designs and a blue line trim under the glaze. All the pieces are reticulated. There are six pieces to this little serving set. $75-125.

    Four footed rim dishes 2.25" to 3" top diameter,
    One plate 3" diameter,
    One basket 1.75" by 2.5".

This German porcelain dessert set is decorated with decals of fruits, pears, grapes, cherries and plums. Blue shaded edges complete the decoration. $300-400.

    Two compotes 2.75" high by 3.87" diameter,
    Two serving dishes,
    Five plates 2.75" diameter.

To set a formal table you would need a centerpiece or table ornament for a floral arrangement. This white earthenware set has two long pieces, two rounded-end pieces and a center cupid on a world globe. It is marked "GERMANY." $350-450.
    Two rectangle pieces 5" long by 2" high,
    Two curved end pieces 4.25" long,
    Cupid on a globe 4.25" high.

A child's cracker jar is a rare item. The background on this German piece is sky and clouds with three children in the foreground. $250-350.
    Cracker jar 4.75" high by 4.25" diameter.

A jardinière is a French term for a vessel to hold plants or flowers. These two jardinières are different styles from Germany, dating from the twentieth century. The green and white set is shaded with a gold rim on top of the stand. The blue and white set has an unusual base, decorated with a decal of a man and woman in period costumes. Each set $65-100.
    Both jardinières 6" high.

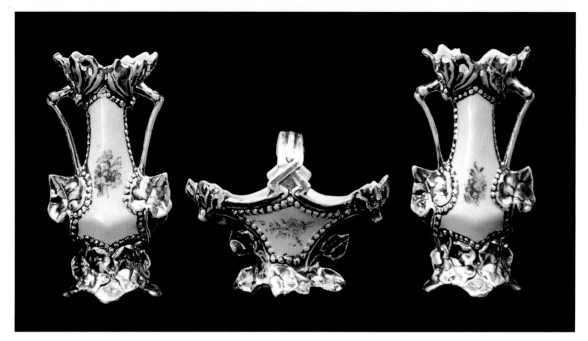

Another mantel shelf garniture set is German porcelain decorated with a small floral spray in the center and gold trim. Some of the gold shows wear. Only the fronts are decorated. They have a Victorian look dating late nineteenth century. $75-100.
Two vases 4.6" high,
Center piece 3" high by 4" wide.

Mantel shelf garniture were a set of porcelain vases to decorate the mantel shelf. In adult size the number varied from three, five, or seven pieces. In the toy size there are usually three pieces. The toy sets were first made in China, then in Holland (in blue and white delftware), and the European countries. This set is porcelain, probably German. It is cobalt blue with raised flowers and a butterfly then painted in colors with a gold trim. $75-100.
Vases 3.25" high,
Center piece 2.25" high by 4" wide.

This mantel shelf garniture set has been combined from two different sets. The vases match but the centerpiece daoesn't. They are German porcelain with a center floral design and gold trim. $50-75.
Two vases 3.25" high,
Center piece 1.75" high by 4.5" wide.

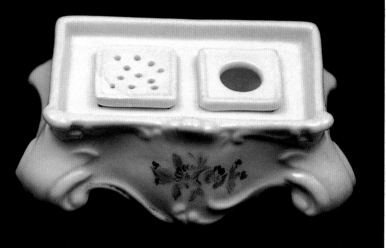

An inkwell is an interesting item for a child's desk accessory. This inkwell is porcelain with two removable containers for ink and drying powder. The front is decorated with a floral spray. Dating is early 1900s. $85-125.
    Inkwell 1.25" high,
    Base size 2.25" by 4".

This miniature ceramic lamp is marked "Dresden." It is beautifully made porcelain with applied flowers and leaves. The base is brown with three cupids holding the bottom portion. $600-800.
    Base 4.75" diameter,
    Ceramic base 5.25" high,
    Metal 2.75" high,
    Chimney 9.25" high.

Inkwells are quite rare in child size. These two inkwells have marvelous covers. One shows a boy with a dog and the other is a girl with a swan. Each $300-400.
    Ink stand 2.25" high, 2.75" wide, 1.62" deep.

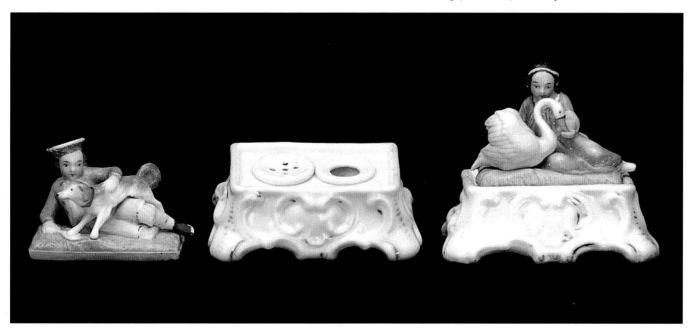

E.S. Prussia stands for the Erdmann Schlegelmilch factory. This washstand set features the four seasons transfers that were used by this company. The scenes show a lady with a flower crown, daisies, autumn leaves, and a holly wreath. This set is exceptional with green background and decals of the ladies of the four seasons. $800-1200.

   Pitcher 5.5" high,
   Washbowl 3.75" diameter,
   Potty 3.75" high,
   Covered soap dish 3.12" long,
   Covered toothbrush dish 5" long,
   Small open dish for sponge,
   Small cup.

German wash stand sets are a nice accessory for a setting. This one is porcelain, decorated with a floral bouquet and light blue edging. Gold rims and trim complete the set. $250-300.

   Pitcher 6" high,
   Bowl top 5.75" diameter,
   Toothbrush holder 1.25" by 3.5",
   Soap dish 1.75" by 2.25".

This is a fine quality washstand set with a serpent handle on the pitcher. It is unique to find this many pieces to one set. Notice the small potty that is out of proportion compared to the other pieces. The set has a beige band with floral trim. $500-600.

   Pitcher 5.62" high,
   Washbowl 2.25" high by 7" diameter,
   Soap dish, toothbrush holder,
   Two covered jars, potty.

German manufacturers made porcelain washstand sets in different shapes and patterns. This set is decorated with blue hand-painted leaves and gold trim. It is nice to have the potty, the soap dish, and the toothbrush holder. $300-400.

Washbowl 5.75" top diameter by 2" high,
Pitcher 6" high to top of handle,
Potty 2.75" top diameter by 2.25" high,
Covered soap dish 1.75" by 2.5",
Toothbrush holder 1.5" by 3.75".

Washstand sets came in a variety of patterns and this one is unique with its decorations of frogs. It shows a frog is sitting on a water lily pad in a pond with cattails and other vegetation. The border is light green. It is German porcelain dating about the early 1900s. $400-600.

Wash bowl 7.5" diameter,
Pitcher 5.5" high,

Small cup 1.6" high,
Covered soap dish with strainer 2.75" by 3.87",
Strainer 1.5" by 2",
Bowl for sponge 3.12" diameter,
Toothbrush holder 2.5" by 5.12".

The theme on this washstand set is Buster Brown and Tige. This German washstand set, circa 1920s, was made for the American market with an American flag. Richard F. Outcault created the comic character of Buster Brown and his dog Tige that began in 1902. $500-600.

    Bowl 6.12" diameter,
    Pitcher 5" high,
    Potty 2.12" by 3" top diameter,
    Toothbrush 1.5" by 4.75",
    Soap dish 2.25" by 3".

Germany made some interesting washstands or chamber sets. The shapes of this one are unique. It is white porcelain decorated with a green border trim, and gold rims and handles. The covered toothbrush holder and oval covered dish have air holes in the covers. $400-500.

    Pitcher 4.5" high,
    Bowl 1.87" high by 5.25" diameter,
    Toothbrush holder,
    Covered dish, potty,
    Slop jar 2.75" high.

This spice set is marked "GERMANY" in a circle. It is decorated with a black band and little pink roses. The large containers are for Coffee, Tea, Sugar, Rice, Barley, and Prunes. The small containers are for Allspice, Cloves, Ginger, Mustard, Nutmeg, and Pepper. A salt box and bottles for Vinegar and Oil complete the set. $400-500.

    Large containers 3.75" high,
    Small containers 2.5" high,
    Salt box 3.25" high,
    Vinegar & oil bottles 3.5" high.

In the early twentieth century German ceramic Koffee (coffee) grinders were made for little girls just as the large ones were made for mother. These are similar in size, with wooden backboards, ceramic holders, metal grinders and glass containers for the coffee. Each $400-500.

Black backboard with a boy and girl decal, 7" high by 2.75" wide.
Beige backboard with green ceramic holder, 6.75" high by 2.75" wide.
White backboard with white orange trim, 6" high by 2.5" wide.

This small canister set is impressed "GERMANY" on the back, near the bottom. The blue Dutch scenes picture all different ships and windmills. It is a charming set in a smaller size dating around 1880s. The large containers are for Coffee, Tea, Flour, and Sugar. The smaller containers are for Allspice, Cinnamon, Ginger, and Pepper. The tall bottles are for Vinegar and Oil. $400-500.

Vinegar & oil 3" high,
Large containers 2.25" high,
Small containers 1.5" high.

German "Blue Onion" porcelain pieces are very desirable for the play kitchen. They were popular in the late 1800s and into the early 1900s. They did come in several sizes. Rolling pin $300-350. Bread board $250-275. Mortar and pestle $125-175.

Rolling pin 3.75" long, with handles 5" long,
Bread board 2.12" by 3.5",
Mortar 1.75" high, 2" top diameter,
Pestle 3.12" long.

Hungary

Hungary had a few pottery and porcelain factories. The best known is the Herend factory, which was established in 1839. It is operated by the Hungarian State. New wares are being made there now. They produce fine quality porcelain and decorate beautifully.

711-2-00/WB
5
J 99

The Herend factory in Hungary is operated by the Hungarian State. Since 1945 the factory produced tableware and tea sets decorated in the classic Herend style. "Herend" is the trademark printed in blue. The decoration is blue underglaze with gold over the glaze. It is a floral design with a stylized pattern. The flower finial is exceptional, with each petal applied by hand. There is gold on all the accents. This is a quality set in fine porcelain. This set was purchased in Hungary in the 1990s. $700-900.
Teapot 3.75" high,
Creamer
Open sugar bowl 3.25" high,
Two cups and saucers 4.5" diameter.

"Herend, Hungary" is on the trademark. This factory produces quality porcelain tea sets, beautifully decorated. The mold has beading. It is decorated with dark green bands, a center rose with green leaves, and a molded rose finial. $700-900.

Tray 12.5" diameter,
Teapot 5.75" high,
Creamer and open sugar bowl,
Two cups and saucers 4.5" diameter.

"HEREND" is the trademark on this covered dish. The porcelain is fine with attractive decorations. It is the size of a child's tureen, but it's doubtful that this was the intended purpose since there is no cut out for a ladle. It is a covered dish with a half lemon for the finial. A slice of lemon with green leaves is on the cover along with a lemon peel. The other decorations are little floral patterns. It could be used for a lemon sauce or lemon slices. $100-150.

Covered dish 3.75" by 5.5".

Since 1945 the Herend factory has produced tableware and tea sets decorated in the classic Herend style. These small lovely pieces may be a butter pat and toothpick holder. Herend factory makes fine porcelain. "Herend" is impressed and the trademark is blue. $40-65.

Small dish 3.75" diameter,
Toothpick holder or vase 2" high.

India

"Dadoos" is the trademark on this tea set from India dating about the 1990s. It is bone china decorated with decals of THE THREE BEARS, which is written on the face of the pieces. The teapot and plate have all three bears, the sugar bowl has Papa bear, the creamer has Mama bear, and the cups and saucers picture baby bear. $200-300.

> Teapot 3.6" high,
> Creamer 2" high,
> Sugar 2.5" high,
> Four plates 3.87" diameter,
> Four cups and saucers 3.37" diameter.

This pitcher and bowl with one covered dish is fine bone china. It is nicely decorated with gold bands and gold trim around the molding and the finial. The decal decoration is pink flowers with beige leaves, over a black band. The style and quality make it look English but the trademark on the bottom reads: "Dadoos, BONE CHINA, Made in India." Great Britain signed the Pitts India act in 1784 and granted India independence in 1947. These sets were sold by Dollmasters in the 1990s. $63-100.

> Pitcher 5" high,
> Bowl 5.25" diameter,
> Cover 3.75" by 2.5".

"DADOOS, Bone China, Made In India" is the trademark. Dollmasters sold this washstand set in 1998. It is a nice size for child's play. The set is nicely made and decorated. $63-100.

> Pitcher 5.25" high,
> Bowl 5.25" diameter,
> Tumbler 3.12" high,
> Sponge bowl 3.25" high,
> Covered soap dish 2.5" by 3.5".

Italy

"GINORI" is marked on each piece. It is from the factory near Florence, Italy. There is a large tray to hold the tea set. It is all white, decorated with embossed figures of a woman. It is beautifully molded in thin fine porcelain. The tray is heavy porcelain. $500-600.

   Tray 9" by 12",
   Teapot 5.25" high,
   Creamer 2.5" high,
   Sugar 2.87" high,
   Two cups and saucers 4" diameter.

"Richard Ginori, Italy, Finest In China Since 1735" is the information given on the trademark. It is from the Doccia factory near Florence established in 1735. In 1896, Marchese Carlo II Ginori went into partnership with Jules Richard of Milan. The firm became Societa Ceramica Richard and Ginori. This is a twentieth century tea set. It is excellent porcelain decorated with a gold band and deep royal blue band with gold rims. $400-500.

   Teapot 4.75" high,
   Creamer 4" high,
   Sugar 3" high,
   Four cups 2" high,
   Four saucers 4.25" diameter.

Italy is a country that had, and still has, many pottery and porcelain factories, but it is difficult to find the children's play dishes. "Nove" is the trademark for a pottery factory in Italy. This plate dates in the late 1800s or early 1900s. The plate is pottery, decorated with green leaves and raspberries. The border trim is blue. It is 5 inches in diameter. $25-35.

The little vase, marked "ITALY," is typical of the wares made for the tourist trade. It is decorated in blue-green, blue and yellow colors. It is 3 inches tall. $10-15.

Laveno, Italy, is the factory known as Societa Creamica, Italiana. This earthenware set has a very nice trademark but there is very little information on the company, other than it began in 1856 and continues to the present time. The company makes table services, vases and luxury porcelain. This set was more likely a demitasse set rather than a child's play set. It has a 1930s design in an orange color. $150-250.

    Coffee server 6.25" high,
    Creamer and covered sugar bowl,
    Eight cups and saucers 4.25" diameter.

The Doccia factory near Florence was established in 1735. These pieces are trademarked "Richard Ginori, Italy" "Finest in china since 1735." These are 20th century pieces. The porcelain is beautifully crafted and decorated with flowers and fruits. They may be condiment dishes to an adult set, but the size fits with the children's dishes. $25-40 each.

    Dish 3.5" by 4.75",
    Square dish 3.5".

Japan

Large quantities of Japanese play dishes were imported to the United States after World War I in 1918 and before Japan's involvement in World War II in 1941. Japanese dishes marked "Nippon" were produced for export from approximately 1890 to 1921. In 1921, the word "Nippon" was changed to "Japan." In 1941, after Japan bombed Pearl Harbor, all exportation to the United States stopped. After the war, Japan was occupied from September 9, 1945 to April 28, 1952. In August 1947, Japan resumed exporting to the United States. Some of these wares were marked "Occupied Japan." Some Noritake wares of this time period were marked "Rose China." Today, Japan continues to make children's porcelain tea sets, usually marked "Made In Japan." The most famous Japanese china factory, Noritake, began in 1904 in Nagoya, Japan for the purpose of exporting.

Factories that made tea sets for export quite often included dinner serving pieces to match. Some extra pieces may have included a covered serving dish, a platter, open dishes, a gravy boat, a serving plate, and salt and pepper shakers. One feature that usually distinguishes a tea set made in Japan is the shape of the cup. It is a low round shape, with a plain loop handle. It comes large, or small, in fine quality porcelain to heavy porcelain, but usually with the same shape.

Most of the dishes that are luster or have luster rims seem to have been made before December 1941. After the occupation in 1952 the rims were usually painted.

Japanese dishes vary in quality from fair to fine, but generally are of mediocre quality. But remember, these sets were made as toys and were priced accordingly. They supplied catalog sales, dime stores, variety stores, department and toy stores. They were intended to be played with and, therefore, are easily distinguished from other fine china.

This Satsuma set is interesting in both the molds and the decoration. The molding is different than anything pictured. It is all hand-potted. The bases of the pieces are uneven. The teapot and sugar are round with uneven bottoms. The creamer and cup bases have six sides and uneven bottom surfaces. The saucer has a swirl of pottery in the bottom. The pieces are made to represent bamboo handles and teapot spout. The decoration is small intricate flowers in enamel colors with gold trim. $600-800.
Teapot 4.5" high,
Creamer 3" high,
Sugar 3.12" high,
Two cups 2" high,
Two saucers 3.6" diameter.

"CHINA, TE OH, Hand Painted, NIPPON" is the information on the trademark. It is called Moriage, which refers to an applied slip used to give a relief motif on the rims of the pieces. This set is decorated with a large red rose with softer greens for the leaves. It would date early twentieth century. $400-500.

Teapot 3.5" high,
Creamer and sugar bowl each 2.75" high,
Six plates 4.75" diameter,
Six cups and saucers 4.25" diameter.

This is a Japanese Banko tapestry-ware teapot dating about 1900. It is a very thin translucent pottery in soft muted colors. There is an impressed mark below the handle for Banko from Ise, a city of the Mie Prefecture (area), in southern Honshu. The city contains sacred Shinto shrines. This teapot is not glazed on the inside indicating it was for display rather than for liquids. The handle faces to the side. $150-200.

Teapot 2.75" high.

Banko is a thin translucent pottery that generally has unglazed exteriors. This set is marked "Souvenir of Kewanee, ILL" on the back of each piece. The iris flowers are hand-painted enamel colors in blue and yellow with green leaves. If they were intended to be used for tea, the inside of the teapot and creamer would be glazed. $300-400.

Teapot 2.5" high,
Creamer 2" high,
Sugar bowl 2.5" high.

"MADE IN JAPAN" is the mark on this tea set. The outline figures are the Sunbonnet Babies, Overall Boys, Cat & Dog. This set has a similar mold as the previous colored set. This set is all blue figures. It would date from the 1920s. $200-300.
 Teapot 3.5" high,
 Creamer and sugar bowl,
 Six plates 5" diameter,
 Six cups and saucers 4.25" diameter.

This early 1900s tea set is marked "Hand Painted Nippon" with a crown. It is quite gray porcelain decorated with a floral design. When you tap the early Japanese sets they sound quite hollow. $200-300.
 Teapot 3.5" high,
 Creamer and sugar bowl,
 Six cups and saucers 4.25" diameter.

"MADE IN JAPAN" is on the bottom of the pieces. This is a common Japanese mold, decorated with Santa Claus carrying a sack of toys. Green holly and red berries are to the left and on the cover. The saucer just has a small decal of Santa Claus. Two pieces $100-125.
 Teapot 3.25" high,
 Saucer 3.25" diameter.

"JAPAN" is marked on this early 1900s tea set. It has thin porcelain, especially the cups. This set tells the story of the Three Bears. Pictured are Goldilocks and the bears with the porridge, chairs, bed, and Goldilocks being chased. Also included is the forest scene with trees, birds and a fox. On another set with the same bear decorations, the baby bear was painted bright blue. $300-400.
 Teapot 3.5" high,
 Creamer and sugar bowl,
 Six plates 5" diameter,
 Six cups and saucers 4.25" diameter.

143

"NIPPON" is marked on this tea set. It is made of thin porcelain decorated with circus animals. There is a black outline and then the figures are hand-painted in colors. This is a standard mold that was used with different decorations. $150-250.

    Teapot 3.5" high,
    Creamer and sugar bowl,
    Six cups and saucers 4.25" diameter.

The original box of this set has "Made In Japan" on the label. The decorations are a little girl with rabbits and other animals, birds, and bunnies with Easter baskets in black silhouettes. The type of porcelain and shapes of the pieces would date the set in the 1920s. $100-200.

    Teapot 3.25" high,
    Creamer and sugar bowl,
    Four cups and saucers 4" diameter.

This porcelain mold is the same shape as the Geisha Girl tea set. This set is decorated with rabbits, musical instruments, and acrobatic scenes. $200-300.

    Teapot 3.5" high,
    Creamer and sugar bowl,
    Six plates 4.75" diameter,
    Six cups and saucers 4.25" diameter.

"NORITAKE, HAND PAINTED, JAPAN" is the information given on this porcelain tea set with serving pieces. It is elegantly decorated with an ivory border, black rims and medallions, all trimmed with gold. The center is white. $400-500.

    Teapot 3.75" high,
    Creamer and sugar bowl,
    Serving covered dish 6" long,
    Sauce dish with attached underplate,
    Platter 7.12" long,
    Serving plate 6.5" wide,
    Four plates 4.75" diameter,
    Four cups and saucers 3.75" diameter.

"Hand Painted, Nippon" is on the trademark. This is a patriotic tea set. The figures represent soldiers of World War I with the American flag, dating this set after 1914. This mold was used with numerous decorations. $300-400.

Teapot 3.5" high,
Creamer and sugar bowl,
Four plates 4.25" diameter,
Four cups and saucers 3.75" diameter.

"NORITAKE, HAND PAINTED, JAPAN" is on the trademark. It is a striking set with large pink decorations, pink rims and trim on the handles. Small flowers complete the decoration on a light cream color background. The center circle is white. The teapot is an especially nice mold for Japanese wares. The set includes twenty-eight pieces. $400-500.

Teapot 5" high,
Creamer 2.75" high,
Sugar bowl 3.25" high,
Platter,
Sauce boat with attached underplate,
Covered serving dish 3.25" by 5.87",
Serving plate 6.5" diameter,
Six plates 4.87" diameter,
Six cups and saucers 4" diameter.

Noritake is trademarked with a "M" in a wreath and "Made In Japan" below that which would date the set after 1921. This is a quality porcelain set. It is decorated with light blue outside and white inside. There is a band of decoration in black with a stylized white and black design. There is gold trim on the rims, handles, and finial. $300-400

Teapot 3.5" tall,
Creamer and covered sugar bowl,
Six plates 4.75" diameter,
Six cups and saucers 4.5" diameter.

"HAND PAINTED, NIPPON" with the rising sun mark is the trademark on this small-sized tea set. The shapes are oval in very nice porcelain. It is decorated with yellow birds, pink flowers and green leaves. $100-125.

    Teapot 3.25" high,
    Creamer and covered sugar bowl,
    Two plates 3.25" diameter,
    Two cups and saucers 3" diameter.

Noritake started using the trademark of an "M" in a wreath in 1904. It was used until 1953. This is an exceptional set of that era in both the high quality and the decoration. It has a white center with a light cream-colored band and green trim. The shapes are more European looking, quite unusual for Japanese wares. $350-500.

    Teapot 4" high,
    Creamer and sugar bowl,
    Serving plate 6" diameter,
    Covered serving dish
    3.25" high by 6" long,
    Gravy boat,
    Platter 5.25" by 7.25",
    Six plates 5" diameter,
    Six cups and saucers 4" diameter.

"Noritake, Made In Japan" is on the printed trademark. This is a nice quality tea set in a smaller size. It is decorated in yellow with a pink band and black rims. The center figure shows the black silhouette of a boy chasing two geese. $300-400.

    Teapot 3.25" high,
    Creamer and sugar bowl,
    Six plates 4.25" diameter,
    Six cups and saucers 3.75" diameter.

"Noritake" with the M is the mark on this cocoa set. It is decorated with outline transfers then hand painted by a real artist. There are nursery rhyme verses on the face of the pieces that include Old King Cole, Little Miss Muffet, and Little Jack Horner. $200-300.

Cocoa pot 4.5" high,
Creamer and sugar bowl,
Four plates 4.25" diameter,
Four cups and saucers 3.75" diameter.

"Noritake" with an M in a green wreath is the mark printed on this cocoa set. A cocoa pot has the spout coming off the top rim. It is a lovely porcelain cocoa set featuring a hand-painted design of a grizzly bear. A light blue and tan background with a tree adds interest to the pieces. $300-400.

Cocoa pot 4.75" high,
Creamer and sugar bowl,
Six plates 4.25" diameter,
Six cups and saucers 3.5" diameter.

The theme of this set, the Phoenix, was a mythical bird that was consumed by fire and rose from the ashes after nine days to be young again. It is a symbol recognized in many countries. Phoenix variations for identification purposes include the names Double Phoenix, Flying Turkey, Flying Dragon, Blue Heron, Howo, Firebird, and Cobalt Bird. Phoenix bird china was in production from the late 1880s until the 1940s with peak popularity in the 1920s. It was made in Japan for export. Children's Phoenix bird sets were made in a number of shapes. This set is rounded, wider at the bottom. The Phoenix bird has dots on its breast. $300-400.

Teapot 3.5" high,
Creamer and sugar bowl,
Four cups and saucers 4.5" diameter,
Serving plate 6" diameter.

Geisha Girls is the theme of this tea set. Geishas are also called Bijin (Japanese Beauties). This Geisha Girl tea set shows seven Geishas in an outdoor setting with a building, trees, and clouds. It is decorated with red transfers then hand painted with colors. The characters' hair is black. Pink, blue, and rose colors make this an attractive set. $200-300.

    Teapot 4" high,
    Creamer and sugar bowl,
    Six plates 5" diameter,
    Six cups and saucers 4.25" diameter.

Geisha Girl is the theme on this dinner set but the pattern is different from the previous set. At least eight different Geisha patterns are known. The patterns are hand-painted in colors with orange borders. The Bijin on these dishes have blue or purple kimonos. It is unusual to find a dinner set in Japanese child's play dishes. Usually we just see tea sets. $400-500.

    Large tureen 3.75" high,
    Underplate for tureen 4.75" by 5.75",

Smaller covered dish,
Sauce pitcher with underplate,
Three platters 3.5" by 4.25" to 4.75" by 6.25",
Six plates 4.25" diameter,
Six plates 3.25" diameter,
Six soup plates 4.5" diameter.

Japan is the maker of this luncheon tea set. It is blue and caramel luster, decorated with a house in an outdoor setting. The handles on the serving pieces are decorated with rose-colored flowers. The finials are a rose bud. The set has a luncheon plate with a ring for the cup. $125-175.

    Teapot 4" high,
    Creamer and covered sugar bowl,
    Four plates 4" by 5",
    Four cups.

"Made In Japan" is printed on the pieces of this set. This is the third luncheon set in this series. It has blue luster trim with a floral decoration. $125-175.

    Teapot 3.5" high,
    Sugar bowl,
    Four plates 5" by 6.25",
    Four cups.

"Made In Japan" is marked on this tea set. The unusual features of this set are the flat front and back of the serving pieces. It has bold coloring on a very light- colored luster background. It is reminiscent of art deco styling. $175-250.

    Teapot 4.75" high,
    Creamer 2.25" high,
    Sugar 3" high,
    Covered casserole 3" by 4",
    Cake plate 6" diameter,
    Six plates 5" diameter,
    Six cups and saucers 4.5" diameter.

Luncheon sets are scarcer than regular tea sets. This is marked "Made In Japan" and would date in the 1930s. The decoration is blue luster, hand-painted flowers in orange and purple with green and gray leaves. There is a rim on the plate for the cup. $125-175.

    Teapot 4" high,
    Creamer and sugar bowl,
    Four cups,
    Four luncheon plates 5" by 6.25".

This bright set is marked "Made In Japan." It is solid pink with blue and green painted decorations and green finials. It is painted in the embossed mold. The shapes are art deco style from the 1930s. The serving pieces have a circle shape but are flat on the front and back. $150-250.

    Teapot 4.5" high,
    Creamer and sugar bowl,
    Four plates 5" diameter,
    Four cups and saucers 4" diameter.

This set is quite typical of wares marked "MADE IN JAPAN" from the 1930s. It has caramel luster, iridescent luster on the bottom of the serving pieces with blue luster on the rims, handles, and finials. It is decorated with hand-painted flowers and leaves. This set is special because of so many serving pieces, including an open square dish. $200-300.

    Teapot 4.5" high,
    Creamer and sugar bowl,
    Square dish 3.25",
    Covered serving dish,
    Sauce pitcher 4.25" long,
    Platter 3.75" by 6",
    Serving plate 6" diameter,
    Six plates 5" diameter,
    Six cups and saucers 4.25" diameter.

This Japanese set is decorated with caramel luster on the bottom half and ivory luster on the top half, with an orange-painted trim. It is hand-painted in bright colors using green, red, black and a blue bird. This type of work was popular in the 1920's up until 1941. $100-200.

    Teapot 4.75" high,
    Creamer and sugar bowl,
    Cake plate 6" diameter,
    Six plates 5" diameter,
    Six cups and saucers 4.25" diameter.

"Made In Japan" is marked on this tea set. It is caramel luster on the base with iridescent luster and gold trim. The serving pieces have an unusual shape, but the cups are the standard shape in very thin porcelain. $100-200.

Teapot 3.5" high,
Creamer and sugar bowl,
Four plates 5" diameter,
Four cups and saucers 4.25" diameter.

The serving pieces of this set have an unusual fluted mold. The background is green luster with a band in ivory luster. The set is decorated with hand-painted flowers and leaves, circa 1930s. The pieces are marked "Made In Japan." $100-200.

Teapot 3.25" diameter,
Creamer and sugar bowl,
Six plates 4.25" diameter,
Six cups and saucers 3.75" diameter.

"Made In Japan" is printed on the base of these pieces. The set is iridescent and blue luster. It is decorated with a calico floral design in red, blue, and yellow with green leaves. It has an unusual shape, flat on the front and back of the serving pieces. $150-250.

Teapot 4.75" high,
Creamer and sugar bowl,
Covered serving dish,
Serving plate 5.75" diameter,
Six plates 5" diameter,
Six cups and saucers 4.25" diameter.

"Made In Japan" is printed on these china pieces, which feature the Kewpies. The Kewpies are the Japanese version of the original Rose O'Neill drawings. The porcelain dishes are decorated with blue luster bands and lids, dating about the 1920s. $400-500.
    Teapot 3" high,
    Creamer and sugar bowl,
    Four plates 3.75" diameter,
    Four cups and saucers 3.25" diameter.

This is a Japanese version of Mother Goose. The figures are colorful in red, yellow and green with green luster trim. It would date about the 1930s. $100-200.
    Teapot 3.75" high,
    Creamer and sugar bowl,
    Four plates 3.75" diameter,
    Four cups and saucers 3.25" diameter.

MADE IN
JAPAN

Little Black Sambo is the subject decorating this tea set. He is walking between some palm trees on some pieces and is watched by another figure on others. The decals are outline transfers with hand-painted colors on a caramel luster background. The handles and finials are colored gold. The cups are very thin porcelain. It is marked "Made in Japan" dating from the late 1930s. $300-400.
    Teapot 4.87" high,
    Creamer and covered sugar bowl,
    Six cups and saucers 3.75" diameter.

152

Little Miss Muffet is the theme on these Japanese porcelain dishes. There are no serving pieces. The set includes grill plates, cups and saucers. They are marked "Made In Japan" and are from the 1930s. $40-60.

    Little Miss Muffet
    Sat on a tuffet,
    Eating her curds and whey;
    There came a big spider,
    Who sat down beside her
    And frightened Miss Muffet away.
    Four plates 4.25" diameter,
    Four cups and saucers 3.75" diameter.

"BETTY BOOP, Des. & Corp. by Fleischer Studios, Made In Japan" is the information given on the teapot of this set. Betty Boop is the cartoon character representing a movie queen of the 1930s. The figures on this set include Betty Boop with blond hair, the animal character Bimbo, and the cameraman Koko. The set is trimmed with caramel luster. $300-400.

    Teapot 3.75" high,
    Creamer and covered sugar bowl,
    Three plates 3.75" diameter,
    Three cups and saucers 3.25" diameter.

"Mary! Mary! Quite-Contrary" is printed on the face of this saucer and cup. It is the heading of a nursery rhyme. It is Japanese porcelain with a green luster border. $10-20.

    Mistress Mary, Quite Contrary,
    How does your garden grow?
    With silver bells and cockle shells,
    And pretty maids all in a row.
    One cup and saucer 4.25" diameter.

"Made In Japan" is marked on this tea set, which is a small version of a Little Orphan Annie set. Annie was a comic strip character created in 1924 by Harold Gray who was a cartoonist for the New York Daily News. The decals on this set include Little Orphan Annie and her dog Sandy. $300-400.

    Platter 3.75" by 5",
    Teapot 3" high,
    Creamer and sugar bowl,
    Four plates 3" diameter,
    Four cups and saucers.

This second Betty Boop set has the same mark as the previous set. This Betty Boop has black hair. The mold is different from the other set and it includes grill plates. It is decorated with caramel luster. $300-400.

    Teapot 3.75" high,
    Creamer and sugar bowl,
    Four grill plates 5" diameter,
    Four cups and saucers 3.75" diameter.

"MICKEY MOUSE, CORP by, WALT E. DISNEY, MADE IN JAPAN" is the information on the bottom of this teapot. This tea set is unusual because it has both caramel luster and blue luster. Walt Disney created Mickey Mouse in the first sound cartoon, *Steamboat Willie*, produced in 1928. This is the earlier Mickey Mouse with a long nose, dating from the early 1930s. The figures are black with hand-painted accents in orange and green. The box is yellow with pictures of Mickey and Minnie Mouse in many different poses. The box reads "COPYRIGHT WALT DISNEY ENTERPRISES, LTD." $700-900.

    Teapot 3.5" high,
    Creamer and covered sugar bowl,
    Four plates 3.75" diameter,
    Four cups and saucers 3.3" diameter.

"MADE IN OCCUPIED JAPAN © W.D.P." is the trademark of this set dating it between 1945 and 1952. The set features Mickey Mouse and Minnie Mouse. The teapot pictures Mickey handing a bouquet of flowers to Minnie. The creamer pictures Minnie Mouse and the sugar bowl pictures Mickey Mouse. The background is black with hand-painted colors on the clothing. $400-600.
 Teapot 3.75" high,
 Creamer and covered sugar bowl,
 Four plates 3.75" diameter,
 Four cups and saucers 3.5" diameter.

Donald Duck is the theme on this porcelain set dating from the 1930s. Donald Duck was introduced in 1934 and had the long bill early on. This is a complete set that came in the original box. It is marked "Made In Japan." The set has caramel luster borders and contains twenty-seven pieces. $600-800.
 Teapot 3.5" high,
 Creamer and sugar bowl,
 Six plates 3.75" diameter,
 Six cups and saucers 3.25" diameter,
 Platter 3.75" by 6",
 Cover serving dish,
 Gravy boat.

Mickey Mouse is the most produced figure from the Walt Disney products. This tea set was "Made In Japan." It is a figural set in caramel luster with red rims. The plates, cups, and saucers have printed figures. The cream pitcher has one ear, which is the way it was made. It is always good to find a set in the original box to know that it is complete. $600-800.
 Teapot 5" high,
 Creamer 3.5" high,
 Sugar bowl 4" high,
 Six plates 5" diameter,
 Six cups and saucers 4.25" diameter.

Walt Disney characters are popular decorations for the children's dishes. This set is marked "IMPORT," which was made in Japan for the European market. It would date from the late 1930s. The set pictures Donald Duck and Pluto the dog. This small size set came in the original box. $100-150.

Teapot 2.5" high,
Creamer and covered sugar bowl,
Two cups and saucers 2.5" diameter.

This Popeye figural tea set was "Made In Japan." Popeye was introduced in January 1929. Other characters were Olive Oyl, Wimpy, Swee'Pea, and Jeep. This set is caramel luster with wonderful figures of Popeye on the teapot, creamer, and sugar bowl. The lids on the pieces are Popeye's hat. The plates, cups, and saucers feature drawings of Popeye and Olive Oyl. This set came in the original box. It is decorated with bright red, green, yellow, and blue accents. $600-800.

Teapot 3" high,
Creamer and covered sugar bowl,
Five plates 3.75" diameter,
Five cups and saucers 3.25" diameter.

"© 1937 W.D. ENT. MADE IN JAPAN" is the trademark on this set's teapot. *Snow White and the Seven Dwarfs* was Walt Disney's first feature-length animated film produced in 1937. The Snow White characters were also used on another mold. This set features Snow White, Doc, Sneezy, Happy, Grumpy, Bashful, Sleepy, and Dopey. The edges are trimmed in light green. It is nice that this set contains extra serving pieces, including a covered serving dish, platter, gravy dish, and a cake plate. $600-800.

Teapot 4.5" high,
Creamer and covered sugar bowl,
Six plates 4.25" diameter,
Six cups and six saucers 3.25" diameter,
Covered serving dish 3.5" by 6.5",
Platter 4.75" by 7",
Gravy base 4" by 5.5",
Cake plate 5.75" diameter.

© 1937
W.D. ENT.
MADE IN JAPAN

"MARX TOYS, MADE IN JAPAN, LOUIS MARX & CO. INC., © WALT DISNEY PRODUCTIONS" is the information given on the trademark of this tea set. The decals are scenes from the story of Snow White and the Seven Dwarfs. The plates each have a different scene. The saucers each show two small dwarfs, and the cups each have one dwarf. $400-500.

Teapot 3.5" high,
Creamer and sugar bowl,
Six plates 4" diameter,
Six cups and saucers 3.5" diameter.

MARX
TOYS
MADE IN JAPAN
LOUIS MARX & CO., INC.
© WALT DISNEY PRODUCTIONS

"MARX TOYS, Made In Japan, Louis Marx & Co., Inc., ©Walt Disney Productions" is on the trademark. This set would date before December 1941. It shows a mix of Walt Disney characters. The figures are Donald Duck, Daisy Duck and nephew, Mickey Mouse and Goofey. The saucers picture Pluto, Donald Duck, Bambi and Thumper. The plates have Donald Duck and Goofy, or Mickey Mouse and Pluto. $400-500.

Teapot 3.5" high,
Creamer and sugar bowl,
Six plates 3.75" diameter,
Six cups and saucers 3.5" diameter.

"WALT DISNEY'S PETER PAN, 23 piece china tea set plus 6 punch-out stand up figures" is information on the box of this set. The china pieces are trademarked "MARX, Made In Japan, Louis Marx & Co., Inc., © Walt Disney Productions." The Marx Company decorated each china piece with scenes rather than single figures. There are twenty-seven different scenes on this set from the story of Peter Pan. Disney released the movie February 5, 1953. In the story, Mr. & Mrs. Darling had three children: Wendy, John and Michael. The St. Bernard dog was Nana. Wendy would tell her little brothers about Never Land where children were forever young. Characters in the stories were Peter Pan, Tinker Bell, Captain Hook, pirates, the Lost Boys, Indians, and mermaids. $400-500.

Teapot 3.75" high,
Creamer 2" high,
Sugar bowl 2.5" high,
Six plates 4" diameter,
Six cups and saucers 3.5" diameter.

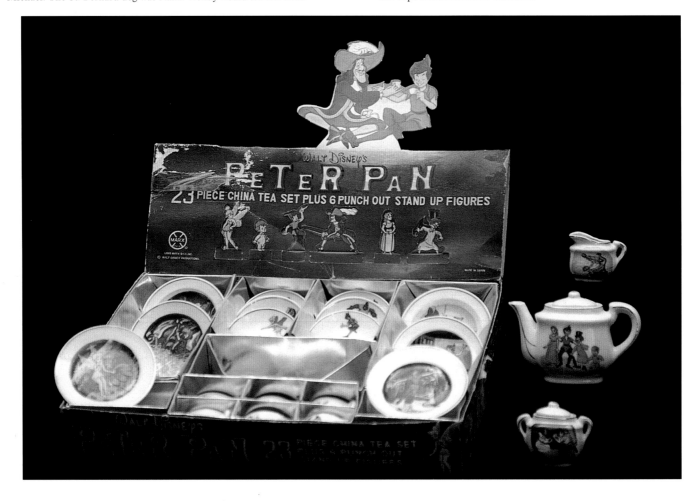

"HAND PAINTED, MADE IN JAPAN" is the information given on this tea set. This is more typical of the wares from Japan circa 1930s. It is decorated with caramel and blue luster, with hand painting of the buildings in the background, the tree branch and red bird. $150-250.
　　Teapot 4" high,
　　Creamer and covered sugar bowl,
　　Four plates 5.5" diameter,
　　Four cups and saucers 3.75" diameter.

"Foreign" is the only mark on this porcelain set as it was produced for the European Market. "CINDERELLA" is written on the face of each piece. This mold was used with different decorations. Here, it is decorated with weird figures representing characters from the story of Cinderella. They are: the Fairy Godmother, Cinderella's stepsisters, the Prince, and Cinderella. This is an old fairy tale but the Disney movie was released in 1950. $200-300.
　　Teapot 3.5" high,
　　Creamer 2.75" high,
　　Sugar bowl 3" high,
　　Four plates 5" diameter,
　　Four cups and saucers 4.25" diameter.

Sunbonnet Babies is the theme on this Japanese coffee and dinner service. This is the Japanese version of the Sunbonnets from the 1920s. Bertha L. Corbett Melchner was the creator of Molly and May, better known as Sunbonnet Babies. She could show character and feelings without showing a face. The Sunbonnet Babies were popular during the 1890s and into the 1920s. This is a large size set for little children to eat real food. The shapes are copies of German wares. The outline decals are the same as the blue set of Sunbonnet Babies. The Sunbonnet Babies are hand-colored in pink, blue and yellow, with overall boys, dog and cat. $600-800.

Teapot 5.75" high,
Creamer 3.5" high,
Sugar 4.25" high,
Six cups and saucers 4" diameter,
Six small plates 4" diameter,
Six large plates 6.5" diameter,
Large covered serving dish 4" high,
Large platter 6.5" by 10",
Square serving bowl 4.75",
Double dish 4.75" long.

"PINOCCHIO" is printed on the face of this teapot. "Made In Japan" is printed on the bottom. The set shows a nice decal of Pinocchio. Other characters from the story include Geppetto, Jiminy Cricket, Figaro the cat and Cleo the fish. The Disney movie was released in 1940. $300-400.

    Teapot 3.75" high,
    Creamer and covered sugar bowl,
    Two plates 3.75" diameter,
    Two cups and saucers 3.25" diameter.

COPYRIGHT 1935
King Features Syndicate, Inc.
MADE IN JAPAN

This is the second set of Annie Rooney. It is smaller in size and has different shape molds. It is marked "COPYRIGHT 1935, King Features Syndicate, Inc., Made In Japan." One saying on the set is "It's Little Annie Rooney and Zero." $400-500.

    Teapot 3.25" high,
    Creamer and sugar bowl,
    Serving plate 4.25" diameter,
    Six cups and saucers 3.75" diameter.

Annie Rooney, the theme of this set, was created by Ed Verdier and Ben Batsford about 1934 for King Features Syndicate. It was a daily and Sunday comic strip created to compete with Little Orphan Annie. This comic strip ended in 1966. The characters included Annie Rooney, her dog Zero, and Mrs. Meany. Books, dolls, and dishes were part of their promotion. These dishes were made in Japan and they also came in a smaller size. The bottom of the teapot reads "COPYRIGHT 1935, King Features Syndicate, Inc., Made In Japan," The trim is orange with decals in bright colors. Each piece has a comic strip saying. The teapot reads "It's Little Annie Rooney and Zero." Other sayings include: "Everything's Gloryosky," "Got The Wim-Wams," "Tea For Two," "Let It Rain," and "Folks are peticlar, Zero." This is only a partial set so there are probably more sayings. $50-100.

    Teapot 5.75" high,
    Four plates 5" diameter,
    Three saucers 4.25" diameter.

"MARY JANE'S TEASET" is printed on the box of this set. "Made in Japan" is printed on the pieces. The figural teapot, creamer, and sugar bowl display the Three Pigs. The other pieces show the Three Pigs dancing with skirts, high-heeled shoes and hats. $200-300.

Teapot 3.5" high,
Creamer and sugar bowl,
Six plates 4" diameter,
Six cups and saucers 3.25" diameter.

"THREE LITTLE PIGS, CORP. BY, WALT E. DISNEY, MADE IN JAPAN" is the information on the base of this set's teapot. The set is porcelain, decorated with caramel luster. The picture shows the three pigs dancing in front of a brick house. Below that is written "THREE LITTLE PIGS." The creamer and sugar bowl have a smaller version of the three pigs. The cups and saucers each have one pig. $300-400.

Teapot 3.75" high,
Creamer and covered sugar bowl,
Six cups and saucers 3.25" diameter.

This Japanese figural tea set is made in the shape of pigs. The story behind this is the "Three Little Pigs." The teapot and creamer pour out the open mouth of the pig. The lids have a flower finial. The bodies have some hand-painted yellow accents, pink noses and ears, brown hoofs and black eyes. The cups and saucers have a printed pig. The porcelain is poor quality made about 1950s. $125-200.

Teapot 3" high,
Creamer and covered sugar bowl,
Two cups and saucers 4" diameter.

"Made In Japan" is marked on the porcelain pieces of this tea set. It is a smaller set with crude figures of the Three Little Pigs and the Wolf. It has caramel luster bands. $200-300.

Teapot 3" high,
Creamer and sugar bowl,
Four cups and saucers 3.25" diameter.

"Made In Japan" is marked on this tea set. The character is from the nursery rhyme "Tom Tom the Piper's Son." The trim is caramel luster. $150-250.

"Tom, Tom, the piper's son,
Stole a pig and away did run!
The pig was eat, and Tom was beat,
Till he ran crying down the street."

Teapot 3.5" high,
Creamer and sugar bowl,
Two plates 4" diameter,
Two cups and saucers 3.25" diameter.

"Made In Japan" is printed on the base of the porcelain pieces. The set represents the story of the "Three Little Pigs," which is written on the plates and the saucers. It is caramel and blue luster with different scenes of the Three Little Pigs. It would date about the 1930s. $300-400.

Teapot 3.75" high,
Creamer and sugar bowl,
Serving plate 4" diameter,
Four plates 3.75" diameter,
Four cups and saucers 3.5" diameter.

"MADE IN JAPAN" with a circle mark is on this tea set. The figural serving pieces feature Bonzo. The other pieces are printed designs. Bonzo was a puppy dog character of the 1920s and 1930s. It is a large set with place settings for three, plus a cake plate. $200-300.

    Teapot 4.25" high,
    Creamer and sugar bowl,
    Three plates 5" diameter,
    Three plates 4.5" diameter,
    Three cups and saucers 3.75" diameter,
    Cake plate 5" diameter.

"MADE IN JAPAN" is marked on this tea set. It is decorated with a little girl and a bear. The colors are hand-painted over the transfer. Caramel luster and black line trim complete the decoration. The cake plate is especially nice with scalloped edges. $300-400.

    Teapot 3.75" high,
    Creamer and covered sugar bowl,
    Cake plate 4.5" diameter,
    Four serving plates 3.75" diameter,
    Four cups and saucers 3.25" diameter.

"RUDOLPH" is printed on the face of this set's pieces. In 1938 Bob May wrote a story for his four year-old daughter about a reindeer with a bright red nose. He put it in a book for her Christmas present. His brother-in-law, Johnny Mark, adapted the story into a song. Gene Autry recorded this song in 1949. The dishes would date from the 1950s. The tea set features Rudolph with a harness ready to pull Santa's sleigh. His nose is lighted and he is ready for work. The set is nicely decorated with orange trim. It is interesting to have the extra serving pieces. The set is marked "Made In Japan." Another set came with blue clouds painted behind Rudolph. $300-400.

You know Dasher and Dancer
And Prancer and Vixen,
Comet and Cupid
And Donner and Bitzen,
But do you recall
The most famous reindeer of all?

Rudolph the red nosed Reindeer
Had a very shinny nose
And if you ever saw it
You would even say it glows.

All of the other Reindeer
Used to laugh and call him names
They never let poor Rudolph
Join in any Reindeer games.

Then one foggy Christmas eve
Santa came to say
Rudolph with your nose so bright
Won't you guide my sleigh tonight.

Then all the Reindeer loved him
As they shouted out with glee
Rudolph the red nosed Reindeer
You'll go down in history.

Teapot 3.75" high,
Creamer and sugar bowl,
Covered serving dish,
Platter 4" by 6.25",
Three plates 3.75" diameter,
Three cups and saucers 3.5" diameter.

Pussy Willow is the name of this tea set. It is "Made In Japan." It is pink pussy willows on brown stems, with a little pink bear. It is a common Japanese mold but it is nice to have so many pieces, including the salt and pepper shakers. $250-350.

Covered serving dish 1.5" high,
Platter 4" by 6.25",
Salt and pepper shakers,
Teapot 3.75" high,
Creamer and covered sugar bowl,
Six plates 4" diameter,
Six cups and saucers 3.5" diameter.

"Made In Japan" is marked on this figural elephant set. The elephant trunk is extended on the teapot and creamer. The set is an iridescent blue-gray, decorated on the robe cover of the elephants. $150-250.

Teapot 3" high,
Creamer and sugar bowl,
Four cups and saucers 3.75" diameter.

"MADE IN JAPAN" is the information on this tea set dating from the 1930s. It has blue-green luster with beige luster. The handles on each piece have a clown head. The center decoration shows two little girls with balloons. $250-350.

Teapot 3.75" high,
Creamer and covered sugar bowl,
Six plates 4.35" diameter,
Six cups and saucers 3.75" diameter.

This little figural elephant set is colored pink. It also came in blue. The little man sitting on the elephant teapot is a mahout (the keeper and driver of elephants). The mold is embossed and hand-painted in blue and yellow. $150-250.
  Teapot 3.25" high,
  Creamer and sugar bowl,
  Four cups and saucers 2.75" diameter.

"MADE IN JAPAN" is printed on the base of these pieces. The tea set is colored green with floral decorations. The base color is green with blue in the molding. It is done in a style to look like Majolica. $200-300.
  Teapot 3.5" high,
  Creamer and sugar bowl,
  Four plates 5" diameter,
  Four cups and saucers 4" diameter.

"© Walt Disney Prod., Made In Japan" is the trademark on this tea set. The original box reads "Disneyland © Walt Disney Productions, Tinker Bell Miniature Tea Set, Made In Japan." It is a doll-size set. Tinker Bell is the fairy from the story of *Peter Pan*. $10-20.
  Teapot 2.25" high,
  Creamer and sugar bowl,
  Two cups and saucers 1.75" diameter.

© WALT
DISNEY
PROD.
MADE IN
JAPAN

"MADE IN JAPAN" is the only marking on this tea set. It has gaudy decorations to resemble Majolica. It is earthenware with a lot of crazing. $75-125.
   Teapot 3.25" high,
   Creamer and sugar bowl,
   Six cups and saucers 4" diameter.

This little set is unmarked but has the look of a Japanese set. It has a squat style teapot, creamer and sugar bowl. The cup is the typical style that was made for export. The teapot has a reed handle. The colors are green, and shades of brown. Please note the interesting covers. This set is earthenware rather than porcelain. $100-150.
   Teapot 3.75" to top of finial,
   Creamer and sugar bowl,
   One cup and saucer 3.25" diameter.

"M - MADE IN JAPAN" is the marking on this tea set. The whole set is pink, decorated with embossing of angels by an urn, with a floral band across the top. The fancy M may stand for a company or an importer. This type of wares may date about the 1930s. $200-300.
   Teapot 3.6" high,
   Creamer and sugar bowl,
   One platter 5.75" long,
   Six plates 5.5" diameter,
   Six cups and saucers 4.12" diameter.

"MADE IN JAPAN" is marked on this dragon set. It is called a slip-trailed dragon motif. The background is blue luster. This set also came in caramel or green luster. It was popular in the 1950s. The interesting part is the extra pieces that came with the tea set. They include two platters, a covered serving dish, and salt and pepper shakers. $200-300.
> Teapot 3.5" high,
> Creamer and sugar bowl,
> Four plates 3.75" diameter,
> Four cups and saucers 3.5" diameter,
> Two platters 4" by 6.25",
> Covered serving dish,
> Salt and pepper shakers 1.5" high.

"MADE IN JAPAN" is impressed in the bottom of this set's serving pieces. This set is very crude pottery, similar to the pottery wares from Czechoslovakia. It has raised embossings of a rooster and a border of grass. It is hand-painted over the embossing. $200-300.
> Teapot 3.5" high,
> Creamer and sugar bowl,
> Six plates 5.25" diameter,
> Six cups and saucers 3.75" diameter.

"Made In Occupied Japan" is printed on these pieces, dating the set between 1945 and 1952. This is in the standard Blue Willow pattern. It is the same shape as the two following sets in green and red. This set is interesting with the extra serving pieces. $250-350.
> Teapot 3" high,
> Creamer and sugar bowl,
> Serving plate 4.75" diameter,
> Covered serving dish,
> Platter 3.75" by 6.25",
> Six plates 3.75" diameter,
> Six cups and saucers 3.25" diameter.

The Willow pattern is one of the best-known patterns that have been made over a long period of time. These sets are marked "TERABAYASHICHINA, OCCUPIED JAPAN." They would date between 1945 and 1952. It is unusual to find them in the colors red or green. They usually came in blue. Each set $150-250.

    Teapot 3" high,
    Creamer and sugar bowl,
    Four cups and saucers 3.5" diameter.

There are numerous sets only marked "Made In Japan" that are nicely decorated. This set has a brown and beige stylized border. The center is iridescent and decorated with sprays of flowers. The nice extras include a serving plate and a covered serving dish. $150-250.

    Teapot 4.75" high,
    Creamer and sugar bowl,
    Serving plate 6" diameter,
    Covered serving dish,
    Six plates 5" diameter,
    Six cups and saucers 4.25" diameter.

This is a nice set marked "Made In Japan." The shapes of the teapot, creamer, and sugar bowl are more unusual for Japanese wares. It is nice to have the extra serving pieces. It is decorated with a soft floral pattern and gold trim. $200-300.

    Teapot 3.25" high,
    Creamer and sugar bowl,
    Platter 4.5" by 6.75",
    Gravy boat,
    Covered serving dish,
    Six plates 5" diameter,
    Five cups and saucers 4.5" diameter.

Some Japanese company produced these doll dishes about 1915. There are no trademarks. It is interesting to see that they came in at least three sizes. They have nicely painted faces. They all have red-orange lids, blond hair, light green spouts and handles. These sets came packaged with three or four place settings. Each set $100-200.

DOLLY TEA SET
"Here's a tea set for your
Dolly and for you.
And greetings for you both
Go with it, too."

Teapots 3.25", 2.75", & 2" high,
Creamers and sugar bowls,
Cups and saucers.

"Toy Tea Set" and "JAPAN" are printed on the original box. This set is in the fruit theme. It has red strawberries with green leaves, trim and saucers. $50-100.

Teapot 1.75" high,
Creamer and sugar bowl,
Three cups and saucers 2" diameter.

"Little Hostess Set" and "Tea Set Made In Japan" is the information on the box. The set is in the shape of a water lily plant and leaf. The really fun part of this small set is a green frog as finials. $75-150.

Teapot 2.5" high
Creamer and sugar bowl,
Two cups and saucers
2.75" diameter.

"JAPAN" is impressed on the bases of this set. This little ceramic set came in the original box with three place settings. It is in the shape of a pumpkin with green handles, spouts and finials. The saucers are green with embossed leaves. They have the look of Majolica. $75-125.
    Teapot 2" high,
    Creamer and covered sugar bowl,
    Three cups and saucers 2" diameter.

"Made in Japan" is marked on these fruit theme pieces. This small set is in the shape of an orange, made of textured porcelain. $50-100.
    Teapot 2.5" high,
    Creamer and sugar bowl,
    Three cups and saucers 2" diameter.

"Fairylite Toy Teaset" and "Made In Japan" are printed on the original box. This is another small set in the fruit theme. This set is in the shape of a yellow lemon with green leaves, and green border on the saucers. $75-125.
    Teapot 2" high,
    Creamer and sugar bowl,
    Four cups and saucers 2" diameter.

This Japanese set is a tiny ninety-five-piece set that came in the original box. It has a small oriental trademark. The background color is deep burnt orange around a white floral design. Dating may be about 1950s. The box size is 11.5 inches wide by 3.75 inches deep by 2.25 inches high. $400-500.

Teapot 2.12" high,
Creamer and sugar bowl,
Twelve cups and saucers 1" diameter,
Soup tureen 1.37" high,

Serving bowl 1.75" diameter,
Gravy boat with tray 2" high,
Two meat platters 2.87" and 3.37" long,
Twelve dinner plates 1.75" diameter,
Twelve soup plates 1.75" diameter,
Twelve pastry plates 1.37" diameter,
Twelve cheese plates 1.25" diameter,
Twelve small bowls 1.12" diameter.

"China Toy Tea Set" is written on this box. It is "Made In Japan." The style of the box and decoration would date this set from the 1950s. It is decorated with a large rooster with a colorful tail. $100-150.

Teapot 3.5" high,
Creamer and sugar bowl,
Four plates 3.5" diameter,
Four cups and saucers 3" diameter.

"MADE IN OCCUPIED JAPAN" is the information printed on these pieces. This would date the set between 1945 and 1952. It is decorated with light and dark blue bands, little floral sprigs, and gold rims. This is a small-sized set, perfect for a doll setting. $100-150.

Teapot 2" high,
Creamer and covered sugar bowl,
Six plates 2.5" diameter,
Five cups and saucers 1.8" diameter.

"Chubo China - Made In Occupied Japan" is the information on this tiny tea set. The American occupation dates from 1945 to 1952. The set is beautifully molded and decorated with tiny gold beading and gold painting. There are little hand-painted flowers on each piece. $300-400.

    Tray 3.75" diameter,
    Teapot 3.4" high,
    Creamer and sugar bowl,
    Two cups and saucers 4.25" diameter.

"Maruichi" and "REG'D NO. 32-4496" are printed on this set's box but the ceramic pieces are not marked. This is a tiny set that was brought back to the United States by a military serviceman in 1960. It is decorated with little flowers. It includes place settings for six people, seven pieces per place setting, plus thirteen serving pieces for a total of fifty-five pieces. There are three sizes of plates, and two sizes of bowls, along with cups and saucers. It would be a wonderful setting with the right size dolls. $300-400.

    One covered serving dish,
    Sauce boat,
    Two serving dishes,
    Three platters 2.5", 2.8", and 3.3" long,
    Teapot 1.3" high,
    Creamer and sugar bowl,
    Six plates 2.12" diameter,
    Six plates 1.6" diameter,
    Six plates 1.4" diameter,
    Six soup bowls 1.6" diameter,
    Six fruit bowls 1.25" diameter,
    Six cups and saucers.

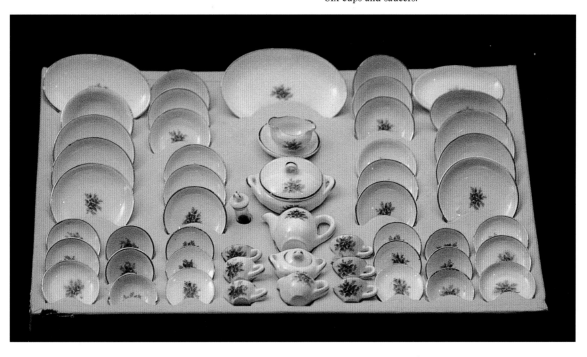

"MADE IN JAPAN" is the information on this tea set. It could be considered either a coffee or tea set. This Japanese set looks like it would be perfect to use in the kitchen with the matching kitchen set of the next set. The decoration includes wide red bands and small blue lines to make it look like plaid. The cups are the usual common shape in Japanese wares. $150-250.

Teapot 5" high,
Creamer and covered sugar bowl,
Six plates 5" diameter,
Six cups and saucers 4.25" diameter.

This kitchen set matches the previous tea set. It is red plaid, marked "JAPAN." It is decorated on the front but the back is white. It is wonderful to find it in the original box and know that it came with thirty-six pieces. $400-500.

Three graduated mixing bowls,
Two serving platters 2.5" by 4",
Cake plate with dome and server,
Two oval pitchers with covers,

Milk and cream pitchers with covers,
Cookie jar and cover with wicker handle,
Serving plate with wicker handle,
Serving plate 4" diameter,
Teapot with lid and trivet,
Smaller teapot with stacking creamer and sugar with cover and trivet,
Three oval graduated canisters with covers,
One little square salt box with cover.

The original box of this tea set reads: "Lady Ballerina Musical Tea Set, Watch her Dance, ©General IND. NY, Made In Japan." The ballerina on the teapot turns around with a music box in the base of the teapot. It would date about the 1960s. The set originally sold for $4.97. $125-175.

Teapot 6.75" high,
Creamer and sugar bowl,
Six plates 4.25" diameter,
Six cups and saucers 4" diameter.

In 1964, this tea set was given to Beth Wylie when she was five years old. It was made in Japan. The musical teapot plays "Tea for Two." It is decorated with red roses and green leaves. $150-250.

Teapot 4.5" high,
Creamer and sugar bowl,
Six plates 3.75" diameter,
Six cups and saucers 3.5" diameter.

"Made In Japan" is printed on the base of these pieces which feature Huckleberry Hound decorations. Huckleberry Hound was a cartoon character from the early 1960s. He is fishing, in the scenes on this tea set. $200-300.
 Teapot 3.5" high,
 Creamer and covered sugar bowl,
 Six plates 3.5" diameter,
 Six cups and saucers 3" diameter.

The trademark on this set has the information "TOYS, FAO Schwartz, Japan." It was made for the toy retailer FAO Schwartz Company. This is a new set from the 1990s. It is decorated with pine cones, greenery and gold trim. It has nice shapes for Japanese wares. $125-200.
 Teapot 5" high,
 Creamer and sugar bowl,
 Four plates 5" diameter,
 Four cups and saucers 4.5" diameter.

This tea set is a modern shape for the 1960s. It is decorated with blue flowers, gray leaves, and red dots. It is marked "Made In Japan." $75-150.
 Teapot 4" high,
 Creamer and sugar bowl,
 Four plates 4.5" diameter,
 Four cups and saucers 3.75" diameter.

"Minnie N Me" and "Toy China Tea Set, Made In Japan" are the information on this set's box. "©Disney" is on the face of the plates. This set is decorated in bright colors of pink, green and yellow. It is from the 1990s, $50-100,
Teapot 2.75" high,
Creamer and sugar bowl,
Four plates 3.5" diameter,
Four cups and saucers 2.75" diameter.

"Made in Japan" is printed on the base of this dish. It is a little celery dish in the shape and color of celery. $35-75.
Celery dish 2" by 4".

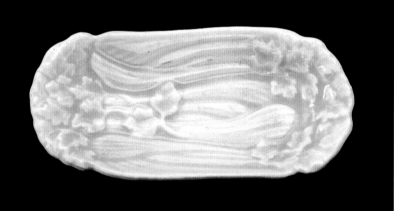

The box of this tea set reads: "Alice In Wonderland, Walt Disney's Toy China Tea Set," "©Walt Disney Productions," "Made In Japan." This is a new set from the 1990s made after companies stopped making the small lids that posed a choking hazard. $25-50.
Teapot 2.5" high,
Creamer and sugar bowl,
Three cups and saucers 2.75" diameter.

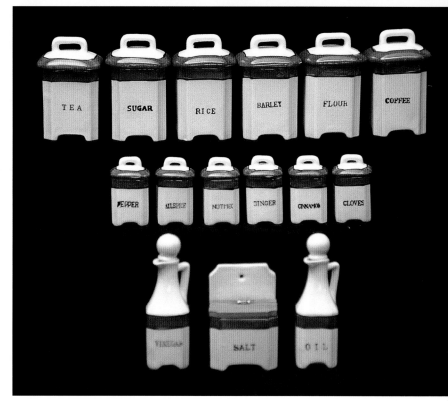

This is a wall pocket that would be hung on the wall to hold flowers. "Mickey Mouse, Corp. by, WALT E. DISNEY, Made in Japan" is the information on the back of this wall pocket. It is decorated with caramel luster and decals of Mickey and Minnie Mouse. $100-150.

Wall pocket 5.25" high by 3" wide.

"MADE IN JAPAN" is printed on the base of this canister set. The large canisters are for Tea, Coffee, Sugar, Rice, Flour and Barley. The small spice containers are for Allspice, Cinnamon, Cloves, Ginger, Nutmeg and Pepper. The tall bottles are for Oil and Vinegar. The salt box has a wooden cover. This set came with an orange border. It was also made with a green border. $350-500.

Six tall containers 4.75" high,
Six small containers 2.5" high,
Oil and vinegar bottles 4.5" high,
Salt box 3.25" high.

The information on the box of this set reads "MADE IN JAPAN," "DRESSER SET – 1 SET." The complete set had six pieces. $150-200.

One oval covered dish 1.62" high,
Small vase 2.25" high,
Covered hair receiver 1.62" high,
Ring tree 2" high,
Fish pin cushion,
Small pitcher 1.62" high.

This tiny washstand set is not trade-marked but has the quality of Japanese wares. It is interesting to see so many pieces. The size is right for a doll setting. $200-300.

Wash basin 3" diameter,
Pitcher 2.25" high,
Sponge dish, toothbrush tray,
Soap dish, pin dish, potty,
Slop jar with cover.

"Made in Japan" is printed on the bases and embossed on the back of each piece. This little spice set came in the original box, which included six containers and four lids. It has a light green glaze over decorative embossing. $75-125.

Vinegar and oil 2.75" high,
Salt box 2.25" high at the back,
Flour, tea, pepper 2.25" high.

The Japanese produced some interesting wares to go with the settings. The vase on the left is decorated with an oriental lady in bright colors. The centerpiece is a covered jar in teal with embossed and colored cherry blossoms. The piece on the right is an incense burner. It is cobalt blue decorated with an oriental woman. Each piece $15-25.

Open vase 2.37" high,
Covered jar 2.87" high,
Incense burner 1.25" high.

Mexico

There are a few children's toy sets that were made in Mexico, but they are hard to find. They are probably more available in the southwest U.S. The quality is usually quite poor. The older sets may have lead in the glaze and would not be safe to use for real food. They are usually marked "Mexico" or "Made in Mexico."

This beverage set is pottery in a blue color. It is not a quality set in either the molding or a true color on each piece. It is the quality of Mexican wares made as toys. A beverage set is unique because of their scarcity. The pitcher is the most interesting piece with a face and stylized designs. The tray has a nice even color with good glaze. The mugs are uneven and need more dark blue color. $150-250.
  Tray 7.5" in diameter,
  Pitcher 4" high,
  Mugs 2" high.

Mexico produced some child size sets as well as miniature sets. I was told this set is from Oaxaca, Mexico, made about the 1950s. It is poor quality pottery. It has a yellow background with uneven brown glaze. It has embossed flower trim on all the pieces. The shapes and sizes are interesting. $100-150.
  Teapot with cover 6" high,
  Sugar bowl with cover 4.5" high,
  Creamer,
  Two cups and saucers 3.75" diameter.

New Mexican Talavera wares are being made in Puebla, Mexico. The Spaniards brought the art of hand-made Talavera to Mexico in the late 16th century. In 1872 Mr. Dimas Uriete bought an old pottery factory. He died in 1916 and his son Isauro inherited the business. He improved the factory and hired artists to bring back the original quality and glaze which gave the pottery its shine and color. In 1990, a group of Mexican businessmen acquired the pottery to protect and maintain its artistic heritage. This set was purchased in 2001. $95-125.
    Teapot 3.5" high,
    Creamer and covered sugar bowl,
    Six cups and saucers 3.5" diameter.

The Netherlands

The Netherlands is also called Holland or one could use the term Dutch wares. Delft pottery had been made in the Netherlands since the 1600s. The main pottery area is located in Maastricht, which is the chief town of the most southern province of the Netherlands. Petrus Regout founded a factory in 1836. His son Lewis Regout established the Mosa factory in 1883. The other main pottery of children's dishes is the Société Céramique. Today there is a great demand for the products made by these factories. There is even a collectors club with 1800 members.

"P.R." is the impressed trademark for Petrus Regout. His factory was in Maastricht, the Netherlands. This set is made circa 1860-1870. There are no matching cups and saucers. There are light brown "spots" on this set. They were made the following way: the earthenware was covered with a thick layer of brown glaze. When the glaze was still wet, the large "spots" were made by pressing a rubber ball to the surface. On the places where the ball touched the glaze, the glaze became thinner and the white color of the earthenware became more visible. $500-700.
 Teapot 3.5" high,
 Creamer and covered sugar bowl,
 Waste bowl.

Petrus Regout & Co., Maastricht, the Netherlands made this tea set circa 1880. It is trademarked with an impressed "P.R." There were no matching cups and saucers. Adults used black sets when they were in mourning, so the children's sets had to be the same. This earthenware set is glazed and has a lot of relief designs. The teapot's lid has a steam hole. In the Netherlands they call these black sets "zwartsten" (blackstone). $500-700.
> Teapot 3.75" high,
> Creamer and covered sugar bowl,
> Waste bowl.

MOSA , Maastricht, the Netherlands is the maker of this tea set dating about 1910. The factory began in 1883. There is a matching dinner service. The trademark is only the word "Décor" and the number "246," both in red. There are also some little marks but they are illegible. The decoration on the teapot is little girls playing with a tea set. Other scenes include a boy and a girl walking a dog, a little boy and girl, a girl with an umbrella, and two girls shaking hands. The decorations on the cups are placed opposite the handles. The handles and finials are very ornate with gold trim and gold rims. $500-600.
> Teapot 4.25" high,
> Creamer and covered sugar bowl,
> Waste bowl,
> Four cups and saucers 4.5" diameter.

MOSA from Maastricht in the Netherlands was the maker of this dinner set. The set is made in good quality porcelain with only some numbers for the trademark. It is decorated in blue and gray sprays of flowers circa 1910. Blue accents and trim complete the decoration. The lid of the soup tureen has a hole for the ladle but there was never a porcelain ladle made by this factory. It has nice handles, with relief. The handle of the gravy boat is a bird's head. This is a junior size set. $500-600.
> Covered soup tureen 6" high,
> Two covered vegetable dishes,
> Gravy boat with attached underplate,
> Round open serving bowl,
> Meat platter, round salt dish,
> Six dinner plates and six soup plates 6" diameter.

This junior set from the MOSA factory in Maastricht, the Netherlands, is the same mold as the previous set circa 1910. The trademark is only the word "Décor" and the number "246" both printed in red. There is a matching tea set to this dinner service. The decals include little girls playing with a tea set, two girls walking a dog, two girls shaking hands while a little girl is hiding behind one of them. Gold trim completes the decoration. $500-600.

    Soup tureen with cover 6" high,
    Two covered vegetable dishes,
    Gravy boat with attached underplate,
    Salad bowl, two meat platters,
    two pickle dishes,
    Six dinner plates, six soup plates
    all 6" diameter,
    Six dessert plates 5" diameter.

The Société Céramique from Maastricht, the Netherlands, is the maker of the matching dinner set dating 1910. This is a junior-size set with the same colorful dressed birds and gold trim. $500-600.

    Soup tureen (missing cover) 3.87" high,
    Covered vegetable dish,
    Salad bowl, two pickle dishes,
    Gravy boat with attached underplate,
    Two sizes meat platters,
    Fruit dish on high stand,
    Six dinner plates and six soup plates
    6.37" diameter.
    Six dessert plates 5.75" diameter.

The Société Céramique from Maastricht, the Netherlands, is the maker of this earthenware tea set. The next set is the matching dinner service. The trademark is the black standing lion dating about 1910. There are many more sets in this mold with different decorations, but you hardly ever see the coffeepot and the waste bowl. The factory used the same cups and saucers for the tea or coffee sets. The decals depict dressed pigeons, cocks, hens and ducks. Gold trim finishes the decorations. $400-500.

    Coffeepot and cover 6.12" high,
    Teapot and cover 4.62" high,
    Creamer and covered sugar bowl,
    Waste bowl,
    Four cups and saucers 3.62" diameter.

"DIV II, Société Céramique, Maestricht, Made in Holland" with a standing lion is the information given on the trademark. Maestricht is the old spelling of Maastricht. A lot of the products have English names. This set is called "Old Dutch." The addition DIV II was used in 1912 and 1913 after the opening of the newly built factory. It is made of earthenware. The transfers are outline transfers, and the colors hand-painted. It's decorated with children dressed in old Dutch costumes, and the trim is a gold rims. $400-500

 Teapot and cover 4.62" high,
 Creamer and sugar bowl,
 Six cups and saucers 3.62" diameter.

The trademark of this set says "Société Céramique, Maestricht, Made In Holland" and has a picture of a standing lion. The lion has a little mark in his tail, at times this tail was changed. This is the key that must be used to establish the date of manufacturing. This mark was used in 1912-1913. The set is made of earthenware and the decorations are silhouettes of hens and cocks on green grass with a yellowish background. It is trimmed with a red band. The next set is the matching dinner set. $300-400.

 Creamer and covered sugar bowl,
 One cup and two saucers 4.5" diameter.

"Société Céramique, Maestricht, Made In Holland" with the standing lion is the information given on the trademark, dating about 1925. The unusual features are the finials shaped like a closed butterfly and the handles shaped like an open butterfly. It is decorated with decals of children: a girl offering a boy something nice to eat and a dog begging; a girl offering to another girl with a dog in the center; and a girl with a cat in a cradle. The rims and extra accents are painted orange. There is a matching tea set with the same butterfly handles. $500-600.

 Soup tureen with cover 5.12" high,
 Two covered vegetable dishes,
 Salad bowl, gravy boat, meat platter,
 Three dinner plates, four soup plates 6.62" diameter,
 Two dessert plates 5.75" diameter.

This is the matching junior set made by the Société Céramique from Maestricht in the Netherlands dating 1912-1913. It features the hens and cocks on the same colored background and trim. $500-600.

 Soup tureen with cover 6" high,
 Covered vegetable dish,
 Gravy boat with attached underplate,
 Four dinner plates, five soup plates 6.37" diameter,
 Six dessert plates 5.75" diameter.

"Delft" and the impressed number "2206" is the only information given on this set. Delft wares have been made in the Netherlands in over thirty five different factories. The name Delft stands for a type of pottery made in Holland. This set is most likely a liquor set but is a perfect size to fit with children's play dishes. It is made to fit on the tray, the cups face right and left with the backs plain white. It is hand-painted in typical Delft designs dating early 1900s. $150-250.

Tray 6" high by 5.75" wide at the bottom,
Carafe 5.75" high,
Two mugs 2" high.

Gouda is an area in the Netherlands where factories make crockery type wares. These are some examples of Gouda wares. There have been some children's sets, but none are available to picture. Some Gouda wares are heavily decorated with a high gloss, or matte finish. They are all hand-painted. The egg cups are marked "FLORA, GOUDA, HOLLAND." They have a matte finish in white, yellow, pink, gray, dark blue, and dark green. They are 1.5 inches high. The little glazed pitchers are samples to show the colors. They are light green, yellow, pink, gray, blue and green, 1.25 inches high.

The covered dish is the size of a child's play serving bowl, at 3 inches high. It is trademarked "1902 Rhone. G.A., PH, GOUDA, HOLLAND." It has an off-white background decorated in blue hand-painted designs. The size is 3.25 inches high, by 4 inches wide. $20-30.

Mantel shelf garniture pieces were made in Holland in delft blue. The top set has a large sailing ship on the front. The pitchers are 3.12 inches high. The center piece is 1.75 inches high by 3 inches wide. $75-100.

The bottom set is a lighter blue with two small sailing ships on each vase. The pitchers are 3.25 inches high. The center piece is 1.75 inches high by 3 inches long. $75-100.

See more mantle shelf sets in the German section.

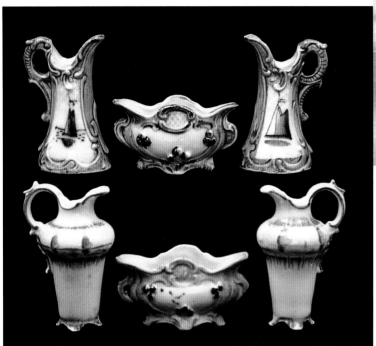

Here are more samples of Gouda wares. They came in all sizes and are hand-painted with a high glaze. The first two plates are 3 inches in diameter; the background is brown to gray. The vase is 3.25 inches high with a brown background and matte finish. $15-25. The two smaller plates are 2.5 inches in diameter with a black background. The prices of each plate would be $8-15.

Poland

Cmielow, Poland established a factory in the late 18th century. In 1848 Prince Xavier Drucki-Lubecki bought the factory. At that time they began producing artistic porcelain. The plant is still in operation. The little set that came on a tray is porcelain, all gold plated. It was produced in the first half of the twentieth century. $75-125.

    Tray 4.75" by 8",
    Teapot with cover 3" high,
    Sugar bowl with cover 2" high,
    Two cups 1" high.

"S M, Chodzies" is the trademark for Stanislaw Manczak in Poland. In 1920, two companies merged. The factory is located at Kolmar in Posen, Poland. This trademark was used from 1928 to 1932. This earthenware set is a version of Snow White and the Seven Dwarfs. The largest covered dish does not have a cutout for the ladle handle. $150-200.

    Large covered dish 3.5" high,
    Covered vegetable dish 2.5" high,
    Large open bowl 4.5" diameter,
    Smaller open bowl 3.5" diameter,
    Sauce boat, platter 4" by 6.5",
    Four soup plates 4.25" diameter,
    Four dinner plates 4.25" diameter.

"S M Chodziez" is the trademark for Stanislaw Manczak from Chodziez, Kolmar, Poland. They used this mark between 1928 and 1932. This earthenware set is decorated with circus and other scenes. They include a clown with a dog, a Native American crawling after a dog, a clown and two geese, a boy with a dog and a man and woman fishing with a large net. The border trim is green. $150-200.

  Soup tureen with lid 3.25" high,
  Covered vegetable dish,
  Gravy boat, meat platter,
  Two sizes open serving bowls,
  Six soup plates and six dinner plates 4.12" diameter.

Stanislaw Manczak from Chodziez, Kolmar, Poland, is the maker of this wash set. It is trademarked dating 1928 to 1932. The set is made of earthenware and the decorations are stenciled. On the water pitcher is the picture of a girl standing in the water holding a landing net, on the wash basin is a boy in a rowboat. Both pieces have green rims. The soap dish and the comb dish have only a green band around the rim. $250-350.

  Wash basin 6" diameter,
  Water pitcher 5.12" high,
  Soap dish and comb dish.

"WIZA - POLAND" is on the trademark. It is a new set from the 1990s. It is an interesting set decorated with blue polka dots. The candlestick is off center to accommodate the handle. The fun part is all the kitchen and baking dishes with the matching tea set. $100-200.

  Teapot 3.12" high,
  Teapot warmer 1.37" high,
  Creamer & sugar bowl,
  Four cups & saucers 2.62" diameter,
  Soup tureen with cover,
  Sauce boat, jug, open bowl,
  Candle holder, pointed baking dish,
  Long bowl, oval serving bowl,
  Four dinner plates 2.62" diameter,
  Four soup plates 2.37" diameter,
  Four spoons 2.37" long.

Portugal

"ANFORA AQUEDA, HAND PAINTED, PORTUGAL" is the information given on this tea set. The shapes are unusual with outstanding bright hand-painted decorations. This set is made of earthenware dating around the 1940s. It has floral trim with some kind of bird. The edges have green dots with a red line on the rims. The serving plates are oval with scalloped edges. $200-300.

    Teapot 4.75" high,
    Creamer 3.25" high,
    Sugar 3" high,
    Two serving dishes 3" by 4",
    One cup and saucer 3" diameter.

Portugal is a country where it is hard to find any children's dishes. These pieces are marked "Anfora Acueda, Hand Painted, 77 Portugal." The 77 may mean 1977. It does not appear to be old. The only pieces available to show are the covered tureen with an underplate. It is decorated in blue and purple. The cover shows a rooster or some type of bird. $20-30.

    Tureen 2.5" high,
    Cover 2.5" by 3.75",
    Underplate 3.25" by 4.75".

Spain

Spain is the country of origin. Although made in a very crude and heavy way, this little set is something special. It was made exclusively for Paula Gerdes by a local potter in a very small town called Naval, in the Pyrenees. The set is decorated with circles of six yellow dots. On the saucers are even three circles of six dots: they are the mark of that town. The clay of the set is dark brown and the glaze is transparent. The shape of the creamer is typical Spanish. $75-125.

 Teapot and cover 4.6" high,
 Creamer and covered sugar bowl,
 Six cups and saucers 3" diameter.

Spain is represented in this little plate. It is earthenware with a heavy white glaze. The writing on the plate is "Restaurante Mediterraneo Paseo de Colon, Barcelona." It may be an advertising piece. It is 3.25 inches in diameter. $10-20

Sweden

"HACKEFORS" is the trademark for J. O. Nilson Hackefors Porselin Aktiebolag from Hackefors, Sweden, circa 1935. The spout of the coffeepot is unusual. Some people call this a chocolate pot. The decorations are of a girl in a pretty dress, on a rock, by the sea, with a fox and with a dachshund. The open sugar bowl and the saucers are decorated with little flowers. The edges are trimmed with a gold band. $150-200.

    Serving pot 6.5" high,
    Creamer and open sugar bowl,
    Six cups and saucers 4.5" diameter.

This set is trademarked "Sju Dvargar, Rorstrand, Co, Walt Disney." It was produced by Rorstrand in Lidkoping, Sweden, in the 1940s. Walt Disney produced *Snow White and the Seven Dwarfs* as a full-length feature film in 1937. The set is earthenware decorated with outline decals and hand-colored. The trim is red bands. Five of the seven dwarfs are pictured with their Swedish names; Butter, Glader, Prosit, Blyger and Trotter. The open sugar bowl has Thumper from *Bambi*. $300-500.

    Teapot 4.5" high,
    Creamer and open sugar bowl,
    Six cups and saucers 4.5" diameter.

Taiwan

Taiwan is the Chinese name for the island we used to call Formosa. It is located off the southeast coast of China. Currently, Taiwanese manufacturers are producing small sets on a tray.

"DISNEY, TAIWAN" is the impressed mark. The box information is "Disney's Beauty and the Beast Toy China Tea Set." The set consists of one teapot and four crooked cups. The teapot is Mrs. Potts, and one cup is her son Chip, with a chip in the cup. The teapot lid is Mrs. Potts' purple hat. The movie came out in the 1990s. $50-100.
    Teapot 5" high,
    Four cups.

"A Mary Engelbreit Design" is printed on the box. It was made in Taiwan. These sets were made to order for Neiman-Marcus department store in the 1990s. This set in the original box comes packaged with place mats and napkins. The decoration is a little girl watering her flowers. She is wearing a black dress and white apron. A similar set featuring teddy bears was also produced using this mold. $100-150.
    Teapot 3.75" high,
    Creamer and sugar bowl,
    Four plates 4.25" diameter,
    Four cups and saucers 3.75" diameter.

Thailand

"Cobalt Net™" is this pattern's name. It has also been called Blue Net and comes from Lomonosov Porcelain, St. Petersburg, Russia, the former Russian Imperial Manufactory. It is also marked "Hand Painted, 22 Carat Gold." This copy of the pattern is marked "Made In Thailang" (for Thailand). It is an earthenware set decorated in blue with gold trim from the 1990s. $50-100.
  Teapot 5" high,
  Creamer 2.25" high,
  Sugar bowl 3.75" high,
  Two cups and saucers 2.5" diameter,
  Tray 8" diameter.

United States of America

Very few play dishes were manufactured in the United States before the 1880s. The majority of play dishes before that time usually came from England, France, and Germany.

Good American china sets are difficult to find. There were many different potteries that manufactured sets of dishes for children. There has never been much mention of the toy wares in the pottery and porcelain books. Some later china sets were made in the 1930s and 1940s.

American sets were usually tea sets with four or six place settings. Sometimes a small waste bowl was added to make the set look English. A large dinner set would include matching tea service pieces. The reason for this was the American custom of serving tea or coffee with a meal.

China play dishes from America were manufactured mainly from the 1880s to World War I in 1914. After that, fewer potteries produced children's dishes. By that time it was cheaper to import dishes from Japan. In the 1930s and 1940s, Depression Glass dishes were made. From the 1920s to the 1980s, tin dishes were popular. From the 1950s on, plastic was the most used material.

As a point of reference, on a box, if there is a telephone number with an area code it would date after 1951. If an address has a zip code it would date after 1963.

"GUERNSEY COOKING WEAR" is the marking on this teapot. The maker was Cambridge Art Pottery, Cambridge, Ohio. The center logo is AP in a large C. From around 1909 to 1924 it was called the Guernsey Earthenware Co. The name comes from the famous Guernsey dairy cows. Guernsey is in the Channel Islands located thirty miles west of Normandy, France. This teapot is redware decorated with black birds or rooks. Three birds are on each side and one is on the cover. $75-125.
Teapot 4.75" tall.

American yellow ware is heavy earthenware dating these pieces from about 1840 to 1870. The pattern is called seaweed. The bowl has a white band with the blue seaweed pattern. The pitcher has a wide lip, and the handle is formed from the body rather than applied. It has blue line trim. The potty is decorated with two blue lines. $600-800.
Pitcher 3.25" high,
Wash bowl 2" high by 4.75" top diameter,
Potty 1.87" high by 3" diameter.

American ironstone wares are interesting because of the weight. This set is heavy earthenware with crazing. It is decorated with a light soft floral spray and gold rims, dating it about 1890. It has a waste bowl to make it look English. $250-350.

    Coffee pot 5" high,
    Creamer and sugar bowl,
    Four plates 5.5" diameter,
    Four cups and saucers 4.87" diameter.

"E L P C O, Made in U.S.A., China" is the information on the trademark. E.L.P. stands for East Liverpool Potteries that were in business in East Liverpool, Ohio, from 1884 to 1903. This was a company made up of six smaller potteries to compete with the larger factories. This set is decorated with elves or gnomes, frogs, scarecrow, a critter, and a crow. It would be a fun set for children. It has the American custom of having serving pieces with a tea set. $400-500.

    Covered serving dish 3.75" high,
    Open bowl 4.25" by 5.75",
    Platter 5.75" by 7.5",
    Teapot 3.5" high,
    Creamer 2.5" high,
    Sugar 3" high,
    Six plates 5.5" diameter,
    Six cups and saucers 5" diameter.

ELPCO
MADE IN USA
CHINA

This set is unmarked but the shapes are an American style, probably from an Ohio factory dating about the 1890s. The serving pieces are oval and the waste bowl is smaller than English sets but was added to make the set look English. The decoration is green transfers of wild flowers called Solomons Seal. $125-175.

    Teapot 5.5" high,
    Creamer and sugar bowl,
    Waste bowl 2" high, 3" top diameter,
    Six plates 5" diameter,
    Six cups and saucers 4.5" diameter.

"ELPCO, MADE IN U.S.A., CHINA" is the trademark for East Liverpool Pottery Company, East Liverpool, Ohio. The company was in business from 1884 to 1903. It is nicely decorated with blue trim. It has one round serving bowl to match the set. $300-400.

    Teapot 3.75" high,
    Creamer and sugar bowl,
    Serving bowl 2" high, 4.75" diameter,
    Four plates 6.75" diameter,
    Four cups and saucers 4.75" diameter.

ELPCO
MADE IN USA
CHINA

"Cleveland China, G H B Co" in on the trademark. The company was known as Cleveland China Co. or George H. Bowman Co. from Cleveland, Ohio. This American company was in business from 1890s to 1930s. The set is decorated with Kate Greenaway figures. $300-400.
    Teapot 3.5" high,
    Creamer and sugar bowl,
    Two plates 6.25" diameter,
    Two cups and saucers 4.62" diameter.

This American set was made by Knowles, Taylor & Knowles from East Liverpool, Ohio. It would date about 1920. The decals tell the story of *Cinderella*. $300-400.
    Teapot 3.5" high,
    Creamer and sugar bowl,
    Six plates 7.25" diameter,
    Six cups and saucers 4.75" diameter.

K.T. & K.
S——V
CHINA

"K.T.& K., S—V, CHINA., P.E." is the trademark on this American set. Knowles, Taylor & Knowles were located in East Liverpool, Ohio, from 1854 to 1931. This set would date from the early twentieth century. It is decorated with Kate Greenaway figures with blue bands and blue trim on the handles. See the English section for more on Kate Greenaway. The shapes are American with large plates and coffee mugs. It could be used for either tea or coffee. $300-400.
    Teapot with cover 4" high,
    Creamer and covered sugar bowl,
    Four plates 6.25" diameter,
    Four cups and saucers 5" diameter.

K.T. & K.
S——V
CHINA
P. E. D.

"T. P. & Co." is the trademark for Trenton Pottery Co. in New Jersey. In 1892 five potteries combined to form the Trenton Pottery Co. This set would date from the turn of the century. It is decorated with decals. The shapes are typically American with a small waste bowl to make it look English. $250-350.
    Tea or coffee pot 5.37" high,
    Creamer,
    Waste bowl 2.12" high by 3" diameter,
    Four plates 4.75" diameter,
    Four cups and saucers 4.75" diameter.

Marjorie Henderson Buell created Little Lulu. Her adventures began in the mid 1930s and were quite popular in the 1940s. Little Lulu appeared in cartoons, comic books, and children's books. The characters included Lulu Moppet, Tubby Tompkins, Alvin, Wilbur Van Snobbe and neighbor children. Little Lulu and Tubby Tompkins are pictured on the teapot, Alvin is on the saucers. These sets also came with just impressed figures and different colored backgrounds. $300-400.

    Teapot 4.5" high,
    Creamer and sugar bowl,
    Four cups and saucers 4" diameter.

The original box has the following information: "16 piece Juvenile set from the Edwin M. Knowles China Co., Newell, W. VA." They were in business from 1913 to 1963 at the Newell factory. This trademark would date this set early 1920s. The mark also has "Semi Vitreous." The set is cream color with a brown wheat pattern. $300-400.

    Teapot 3.5" high,
    Creamer and open sugar bowl,
    Four plates 6.5" diameter,
    Four cups and saucers 4.75" diameter.

This is an American set, circa 1920, decorated with scenes from the nursery rhyme, "This Is The House That Jack Built." There are sayings on the front of the pieces. These decals were also used on German wares. $300-400.

    "This is the horse and the hound and the horn,
    That belonged to the farmer sowing his corn,
    That kept the cock that crowed in the morn,
    That waked the priest all shaven and shorn,
    That married the man all tattered and torn,
    That kissed the maiden all forlorn,
    That milked the cow with the crumpled horn,
    That tossed the dog,
    That worried the cat,
    That killed the rat,
    That ate the malt,
    That lay in the house that Jack built."

    Teapot 4.25" high,
    Creamer and sugar bowl,
    Six cups and saucers 4.75" diameter.

This American set is not trademarked but has the same mold as sets from Bennett Company, East Liverpool, Ohio in the 1920s. The factory closed in 1930. The decals are scenes of rabbits and chickens. The sugar bowl ties them together with both rabbits and chickens. $250-350.

 Teapot 4.5" high,
 Creamer and sugar bowl,
 Three plates 6.5" diameter,
 Three cups and saucers 5.25" diameter.

"Victory, Made In U.S.A." is the trademark on the china. Victory was used on the marks during World War II, 1941-1945. The original box has "Chinaware, Semi Vitreous, PO Box 277, Salem, Ohio." The decals are from the nursery rhymes "Little Boy Blue Come Blow Your Horn," "Peter, Peter Pumpkin Eater," and "Mary Had A Little Lamb." $300-400.

 Teapot 4.25" high,
 Creamer and sugar bowl,
 Four plates 6.5" diameter,
 Four cups and saucers 5" diameter.

Edwin M. Knowles was located in Newell, West Virginia. This set is trademarked "Semi Vitreous, Edwin M. Knowles China Co., Made in U.S.A." It would date around the early 1920s. The set is decorated with a big red rose, green leaves, and red rims. $200-300.

 Teapot 4.5" high,
 Creamer 2.25" high,
 Open sugar bowl, 2" high,
 Four plates 6.5" diameter,
 Four cups and saucers 4.75" diameter.

"Edwin M. Knowles China Co., Made in U.S.A." is printed on the trademark. The set would date about 1942. It has interesting animal figures. There is a monkey with a candy cane and ice cream cone; a pig riding a goose; a hippopotamus roller-skating; and an elephant roller-skating. The teapot mold is more unusual in a squat style. $300-400.

 Teapot 3.5" high,
 Creamer and sugar bowl,
 Four plates 6.25" diameter,
 Four cups and saucers 5.25" diameter

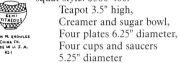

The trademark reads "by Salem China Co., Made in U.S.A., 23 Karat Gold." The design is "Basket Petit Point," one of Salem's most popular dinnerware patterns. It is nice to find this set with the teapot. It would date from the early 1940s. $300-400.

    Teapot 4.5" high,
Creamer and sugar bowl,
Cake plate 7.5" diameter,
Four plates 6.5" diameter,
Four cups and saucers 5" diameter.

"Symphony, by Salem China Co., Salem, Ohio, Made in U.S.A., 23 Karat Gold" is the information on the trademark. This mark was used in the late 1940s. The rims are gold, and the center decorations are Colonial figures. The cake plate is a nice addition to the set. It is 7.25" in diameter and measures 8" in diameter to the ends of the handles. $300-400.

    Teapot 4.5" high,
Creamer 2" high,
Open sugar bowl 1.75" high,
Cake plate 7.25" diameter,
Four plates 6.5" diameter,
Four cups and saucers 5" diameter.

"Sampler by Salem China Co., Made In U.S.A., 23 Karat Gold" is on the trademark. This is the second set with the same trademark and decoration but the trademark includes the pattern name "Sampler." This is an unusual shape teapot. $250-350.

    Teapot 3" high,
Cake plate 7.5" diameter,
Four plates 6.25" diameter,
Four cups and saucers 3.75" diameter.

"Blue Ridge, Hand Painted, Underglaze, Southern Potteries, Inc., Made In U.S." is the information on the bottom of this tea set. Southern Potteries was located in Erwin, Tennessee. The factory began in 1917 and closed in 1957. Their peak period was about the mid 1940s to early 1950s. The company used several molds for the children's wares. This pattern is called "Forget-me-nots." There are soft colors in pink, green, and blue with black stems. The rims are sponged pink. $500-600.

    Serving pot 6" high,
Creamer 3" high,
Open sugar bowl 2" high,
Four plates 6" diameter,
Four cups and saucers 5" diameter.

Another Blue Ridge set by Southern Potteries is decorated in primary colors. The flowers are red, blue and yellow with green leaves and trim. The pattern name is "Lovely Linda." $500-600.

> Coffee pot 6" high,
> Creamer and sugar bowl,
> Four plates 6.25" diameter,
> Four cups and saucers 4.75" diameter.

Blue Ridge by Southern Potteries was the maker of this child's set. The pattern name is "Cynthiana." It is yellow with green leaves and trim, on a Colonial shape. $500-600.

> Coffee pot 6" high,
> Creamer and sugar bowl,
> Four plates 6.25" diameter,
> Four cups and saucers 4.75" diameter.

Blue Ridge by Southern Potteries was the maker of this child's set. It is decorated in a floral design. The colors are rose and gray with green leaves and trim on a Colonial shape. The pattern name is "Whirligig." $500-600.

> Coffee pot 6" high,
> Creamer and sugar bowl,
> Four plates 6.25" diameter,
> Four cups and saucers 4.75" diameter.

The Erwin Pottery Company, located in Erwin Tennessee, was started by Negatha and Earl Peterson in 1957, after Southern Potteries closed. They were able to buy some of the Blue Ridge molds. Negetha was a decorator at Southern Potteries (Blue Ridge). Earl worked there before World War II. The company is still in business with limited production.

This set was made by Erwin Pottery in Erwin, Tennessee. The sugar bowl has the information "Original Blue Ridge Pattern, SPI, Erwin Pottery." It is in the style of French Quimper peasants. The teapot looks like a Blue Ridge mold. It is unusual in that it came with mugs rather than cups and saucers. $300-400.

> Teapot 6.25" high,
> Creamer and sugar bowl,
> Four mugs 3.25" high.

200

"Erwin Pottery, Hand Painted, Erwin, Tenn." is the mark on this American coffee set. It dates after Southern Potteries closed in 1957. It is decorated in the French Quimper style with the man and woman. It has a yellow border and tan decoration. $300-400.

    Coffee pot 6.25" high,
    Creamer 3.12" high,
    Sugar bowl 3.5" high,
    Four plates 6" diameter,
    Four cups and saucers 4.5" diameter.

This Majolica set is not trademarked. It is not a quality pottery set, colored in brown and green. It is in the shape of pineapples. The unusual feature is the cover on the cups. One would wonder if the purpose was to serve pineapple juice. $100-200.

    Serving pot 5.25" high,
    Four cups with covers 3.25" high.

This set is not trademarked and is possibly American made. It was sold by Marshall Fields stores in the 1990s. The finials on the serving pieces are pink ceramic bows. The serving pieces are ivory. The cups and saucers are blue, ivory, and pink. $150-250.

    Teapot 5" high,
    Creamer and sugar bowl,
    Six cups and saucers 4.75" diameter.

"Erwin Pottery, Hand Painted, Erwin, Tenn." is on the trademark, the same as the previous set. The set is signed N.P. for Negatha Peterson. Erwin Pottery work is in the style of Southern Potteries after they closed. This set decoration is reminiscent of French peasants on the Quimper wares. $300-400.

    Teapot 4" high,
    Creamer 2.5" high,
    Sugar bowl 2.75" diameter,
    Four plates 4" diameter,
    Four cups and saucers 3.25" diameter.

In 1895 the Chelsea Pottery in Massachusetts moved to Dedham and changed the name to Dedham Pottery. They were known for producing a gray crackleware with blue decorations. The rabbit pattern was the most popular. They made some children's feeding dishes but there are no documented play dishes. The factory closed in 1943. The Potting Shed in Concord, Massachusetts, made this small tea set similar to Dedham ware in 1997, for the price of about $70.00. The set includes a teapot, creamer, two plates, two cups and saucers that came in the original box. There was no sugar bowl. This set has the crackle appearance of the old wares. $100-150.

> Teapot 3" high,
> Creamer,
> Two plates 3.75" high,
> Two cups and saucers 3" diameter

This set is known as American Colonial. The person that sold the set said it was from the American Ceramic Company located in Sebring, Ohio from the 1930s. It is not trademarked. It has soft pastel colors in pink, blue, and yellow. Please notice the embossed molds. $200-300.

> Server 5.75" high,
> Creamer and sugar bowl,
> Six plates 5" diameter,
> Six cups and saucers 4" diameter.

Fiesta Ware was made by the Homer Laughlin China Company of Newell, West Virginia. It was produced as inexpensive pottery in brilliant colors, starting in the 1930s to the 1970s. They are now making Fiesta ware again with the following trademark.

This child's set was packaged in a box, titled "My First Fiesta®." A new set in the 1990s sold for $86.00.

> Teapot 4.75" high,
> Creamer and covered sugar bowl,
> Two plates 6.12" diameter,
> Two cups and saucers 6" diameter.

The Hall China Co. from East Liverpool, Ohio was founded in 1903. "Autumn Leaf" was designed for the Jewel Tea Company in 1933. This small set from the 1990s has the following information: "Limited Edition, Autumn Leaf, Collector miniatures by China Specialties. Not for food use. May poison food, not a toy." $125-150.

    Teapot 2.5" high,
    Creamer and sugar bowl,
    Two cups and saucers 2.6" diameter.

LIMITED EDITION
Autumn Leaf
COLLECTOR MINIATURES
by CHINA SPECIALTIES
NOT FOR FOOD USE.
MAY POISON FOOD.
NOT A TOY

The Victoria and Albert Museum sponsored a series of six reproduction teapots in 1985. They were sold by the Franklin Mint for $55.00 each. They are marked fine porcelain.

The first teapot is marked "Hochst." It is 3.5 inches high. It is decorated with a castle. The second teapot is marked "Tournay." It has a nice flower finial and is 4.5 inches tall. Two birds and flowers with gold trim make this an attractive set. The third teapot is marked "Koyoto" and is 3.25 inches high. This teapot has a paper label "Made In Japan." Inside the cover is a Japanese cartouche. It is decorated with green oriental leaves and blue flowers. The fourth teapot is trademarked "Bow, Fine Porcelain, © 1985 Franklin Mint." The size is 4.75" high.

"THE GOOSE BASKET" is the information on the trademark. It is a new American set of quite nicely potted earthenware. It has tiny pink flowers with pink trim on a cream-colored base. $50-75.

    Teapot 4" high,
    Creamer and open sugar bowl,
    Four plates 4" diameter,
    Four cups and saucers 3" diameter.

This set is not trademarked, but it should be in the American section because of the material used to make this set. It is ceramic, very light, and hollow sounding. All the bottoms are flat and glazed. Made of poor materials, it would chip easily. It is decorated with floral decals with silver rims, handles, and finials. $50-100.

Teapot 5" high,
Creamer and sugar bowl,
Five plates 6" diameter,
Five cups and saucers 3.75" diameter.

Mary Alice Hadley from Louisville, Kentucky is a potter who produced these wares in the 1990s. These children's dishes are heavy stoneware pottery with a blue teddy bear decoration. Hadley pottery began manufacturing adult services in 1940. The designs were created or suggested by Mary Alice Hadley and are painted free-hand on each piece. The ware is a modified stoneware made of native clays. The decorations are applied on unfired clay shapes, then coated with a glaze and fired. This is also called underglaze decoration. This process makes the decorations very durable. $50-100.

Teapot 4.5" high,
Creamer and sugar bowl,
Two cups and saucers 4" diameter.

"TOM & JERRY, © 1989 Turner Ent. Co., All Rights Reserved" is the information printed on the face of this teapot. The other pieces have two little mice. It looks like an American set. Some Tom & Jerry items were available starting in the 1960s. $150-250.

Teapot 5.75" high,
Creamer 2.5" high,
Sugar bowl 2.75" high,
Four cups and saucers 3.5" diameter.

Mary Hadley also made this canister set in stoneware. It has the same color blue as the tea set. The containers are for flour, sugar, coffee, and tea. It would look nice in a little girl's kitchen. $75-125.

Flour 4.75" high,
Sugar 4.25" high,
Coffee 3.87" high,
Tea 3.5" high

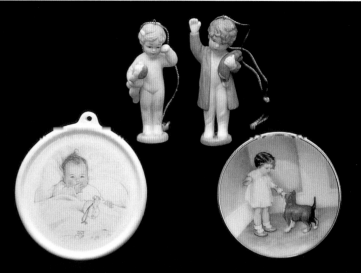

Bessie Pease Gutmann was an American artist, 1876-1960. She was famous for her baby and children prints. Her work included prints, calendars, magazine covers, book illustrations, advertisements, posters and Christmas cards. Her work dates from 1905 to 1947. She retired because of failing eyesight. There were pieces produced in the 1990s that included ornaments, a hanging porcelain picture and a small plate. The baby plate with a rabbit is 3.5" in diameter. The trademark reads "Gutmann Collectors Club, Bessie Pease Gutmann is a trademark of the Balliol Corporation." $10-20. The Reward plate reads "The Reward 50th Anniversary by Bessie Pease Gutmann, ©1991 The Balliol Corporation, Lancaster, PA. All Rights Reserved." The plate is 3.25" in diameter. $10-20.

A child size jardinière is very unusual. It is unmarked but looks like American earthenware. The colors are cobalt fading to olive green. The embossing is rose buds with long stems and leaves. $200-300.

Top planter 6.25" high by 7.75" diameter,
Pedestal 7.62" high by 6.25" diameter,
Total height is 14" high.

This odd little American item is located in the bathroom. The bed pan is trademarked "Judy Kirk, Ceramics, Conneautville, PA. Copyright 1951." It has a little verse printed in the bottom that reads "A bedpan is a toy from hell, so hurry up and do get well." It is pottery with a glaze. The size is 3.25 inches wide by almost 5 inches long. $10-15.

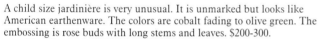

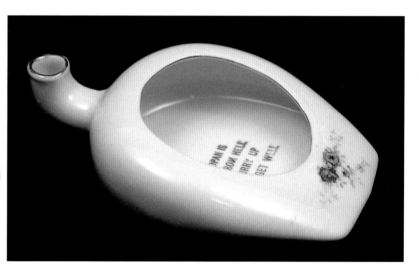

This child's rolling pin is not trademarked. It is American from about the 1920s. The decal is from the poem "Mary Had A Little Lamb." $250-350.

Rolling pin 8.75 inches long plus the cork end.

Bibliography

Andacht, Sandra, Garthe, Nancy & Mascarelli, Robert. *Price Guide to Oriental Antiques.* Des Moines, IA: Wallace Homestead, 1981.

Bond, Michael. *A Bear Called Paddington.* London: Collins, 1997.

Collins, Ace. *Stories Behind The Best Loved Songs of Christmas.* Grand Rapids, MI: Zondervan, 2001.

Godden, Jeoffrey A. *Encyclopaedia of British Pottery and Porcelain Marks.* New York, N.Y: Bonanza Books, 1964.

Grant, John. *Encyclopedia of Walt Disney's Animated Characters.* New York, NY: Huperion, 1998.

Hake, Ted. *Hake's Guide to Comic Character Collectibles.* Radnor, PA: Wallace-Homestead Book Co., 1993.

Kowalsky, Arnold A & Dorothy E. *Encyclopedia of Marks 1780-1980.* Atglen, PA: Schiffer Publishing, 1999.

Lehner, Lois. *U.S. Marks on Pottery, Porcelain & Clay.* Paducah, KY: Collector Books, 1988.

Longest, David & Stern, Michael. *The Collector's Encyclopedia of Disneyana.* Paducah, KY: Collector Books, 1992.

Marple, Leland & Carol. *R.S. Prussia: The Formative Years.* Atglen, PA: Schiffer Publishing, 2002.

Marple, Leland & Carol. *R.S. Prussia: The Art Nouveau Years.* Atglen, PA: Schiffer Publishing, 1998.

Marple, Leland & Carol. *R.S. Prussia: The Wreath and Star.* Atglen, PA: Schiffer Publishing, 2000.

Munsey, Cecil. *Disneyana: Walt Disney Collectibles.* New York, N.Y: Hawthorn Books, 1974.

Newbound, Betty & Bill. *Southern Potteries Inc.: Blue Ridge Dinnerware.* Paducah, KY: Collector Books, 1993.

O'Neill, Ann Marie. *Quimper Pottery.* Atglen, PA: Schiffer Publishing, 1994.

Penkala, Maria. *European Porcelain.* Rutland, VT: Charles E. Tuttle Co., 1968.

Penkala, Maria. *European Pottery.* Rutland, VT: Charles E. Tuttle Co., 1968.

Punchard, Lorraine. *Playtime Dishes.* Des Moines, IA: Wallace Homestead Book, 1978.

Punchard, Lorraine. *Child's Play.* Bloomington, MN: Lorraine Punchard, 1982.

Punchard, Lorraine. *Playtime Kitchen Items and Table Accessories.* Bloomington, MN: Lorraine Punchard, 1993.

Punchard, Lorraine. *Playtime Pottery & Porcelain from the United Kingdom & the United States.* Atglen, PA: Schiffer Publishing, 1996.

Punchard, Lorraine. *Playtime Pottery & Porcelain from Europe & Asia.* Atglen, PA: Schiffer Publishing, 1996.

Reilly, Robin. *Wedgwood: The new Illustrated Dictionary.* Woodbridge, England: Antique Collectors Club, 1995.

Rontgen, Robert E. *Marks on German, Bohemian, and Austrian Porcelain.* Exton, PA: Schiffer Publishing, 1981.

Savage, George & Newman, Harold. *An Illustrated Dictionary of Ceramics.* New York, NY: Van Nostrand Reihold Co., 1976.

Schroy, Ellen T. *Warman's Americana & Collectibles.* Iola, WI: Krause Publications, 2001.

Van Patten, Joan. *The Collector's Encyclopedia of Noritake.* Paducah, KY: Collector Books, 1984.

Zuhlsdorff, Dieter. *Marken Lexikon: Porzellan und Keramik Report 1885-1935.* Stuttgart, Germany: Arnold'sche, 1988.

Index